THE CHRISTIAN—MUSLIM FRONTIER

The Christian–Muslim Frontier

Chaos, Clash or Dialogue?

Edited by

Jørgen S. Nielsen

I.B.Tauris *Publishers*
LONDON ● NEW YORK

Published in 1998 by
I.B.Tauris & Co Ltd
Victoria House, Bloomsbury Square, London WC1B 4DZ

In the United States and in Canada distributed by St Martin's Press
175 Fifth Avenue, New York NY 10010

A full CIP record for this book is available from the British Library
A full CIP record for this book is available from the Library of
Congress

ISBN 1 86064 099 0

Library of Congress catalog card number: available

Typeset in Adobe Caslon by Hepton Books, Oxford
Printed and bound in Great Britain by WBC Ltd, Bridgend

Contents

Foreword

Dialogue of Religions, Dialogue of Cultures

A Message from H. E. Mintimer Sh. Shaimiyev, President of the Republic of Tatarstan

Today the Republic of Tatarstan is rightly considered one of the stable regions of the former Soviet Union. In fact the chosen policy of a gradual transition to a market economy has enabled us to avoid economic cataclysms, sharp falls of living standards, declining production, and agricultural crisis. In general, we have preserved peace in the Republic, and avoided the international conflicts which have such tragic outcomes in many regions.

Since ancient times the representatives of Turkic, Slavic and Finno–Ugrian peoples have lived and worked in peace on the territory of modern Tatarstan, preserving their national features and national originality. The proclamation of the sovereignty of Tatarstan gave a new impulse to the development of mutual understanding, traditions and respect, in a culture of inter-ethnic intercourse which has been established for ages.

Tatarstan is a democratic state, expressing the will and interests of all national peoples of the Republic. At the same time Tatarstan is called to fulfil its role as the spiritual centre of the Tatar community living in the Russian Federation, and in many countries and regions of the former Soviet Union.

At present in the Tatarstan Republic the process of the national revival of the Tatar people is developing: the restoration of the lost state system, the entry of Tatarstan into the international scene, formation of Tatar as the state language parallel with the Russian language, and a return to religion and to the spiritual heritage of the past. Historically two peoples are equally represented in Tatarstan,

Tatars and Russians, and, therefore also the two biggest religions, Islam and Orthodox Christianity. At the same time among Tatars there is a Christian minority (Baptists–Kriashens). Officially Islam was adopted in 922 by Bulgars who were the ancestors of modern Kazan Tatars. After the Kazan Khanate's conquest in 1552 the policy of the Christianisation of the region began and Orthodoxy was proclaimed as the dominant state religion.

The history of relations between Islam and Orthodoxy is full of dramatic contradictions. However in recording its pages and reviving historical objectively we have to do everything possible to avoid mutual historical demands, offenses, and unfairness which could be the ground for new conflicts today.

In the foreign mass media and scientific publications there is a widespread impression of religious revival of peoples in the former Soviet Union. We must say that in our Republic we have the same process: new mosques and churches are being opened, religious organisations are being registered. It is also necessary to say that the religion has no influence on the majority of the spheres of social life. Therefore its influence should not be exaggerated and there is no reason to speak about any possible 'Islamic' revolutions in the near future.

Tatarstan's official policy in religious questions aims at meeting the interests of all ethno-religious groups of the population in order to avoid the creation of any officially privileged religion, as it happens in some republics.

From the pre-revolutionary and the Soviet period we have received a heavy heritage connected with the fact that in the history of our country the religious question has not been solved in democratic ways. This is especially true of Islam. Islam was discriminated against in Tsarist as well as in Soviet Russia. The policy of state atheism crushed the great and unique Islamic culture, which gave to the world prominent poets, scientists and philosophers. At the end of the 19th and at the beginning of the 20th centuries Kazan was well-known all over the Islamic world as a centre of religious reformation, one of the forms of which was Jadidism.

Today we consider that our duty is to revive the religious culture, to return all religious buildings and educational institutions to believers and to assist in the construction of new buildings. In the Republic of Tatarstan Christmas and Kurban–Bairam have been proclaimed as holidays. National religious festivals are widely celebrated. In 1993 a large number of believers made the pilgrimage to Mecca.

But we do not idealise reality. Religion is not only an ideology but it is also a social and political power. The great activity of foreign sects and missions upsets our believers. Their activity is being understood as the destruction of the traditional cultures, as an ideological intervention by Muslim and Christian sides.

In spite of this, freedom of belief means a free choice of an object of belief. Therefore, today in our Republic Lutherans, Hare Krishna and neo-Protestant organisations and missionaries are active.

Our society has rejected totalitarian ideology. It is a positive fact, but at the same time today we see a spiritual vacuum. In these conditions moral and religious values, general ideals, ideas of good, respect, mutual aid, diligence, unity could have a beneficial influence on the people's consciousness.

Religion as a phenomenon of the life of society requires scientific and objective study. For a long time Kazan was a well-known centre of oriental studies. Unfortunately this tradition was artificially undermined. Today it is necessary to revive the Islamic centres in Kazan.

This process has already begun. An International Turcological Conference has taken place and now Kazan is hosting the international seminar on the Christian–Muslim Frontier. We hope that such scientific contacts will make our capital a place of meeting of the West and the East, of Islamic and Christian civilisations yet again.

Acknowledgements

This book is based on the proceedings of a conference on 'The Christian-Muslim frontier: History, Myths and Current Perceptions' – The organisers of the conference – The Institute for African Studies at the Russian Academy of Sciences in Moscow, under the leadership of Professor Aleksei Vasiliev, and the Centre for the Study of Islam and Christian-Muslim Relations (CSIC), Selly Oak Colleges, Birmingham – are particularly grateful to the Edward Cadbury Charitable Trust for providing the funding which enabled the Western European team to attend the conference. We are also grateful to the Tatarstan Academy of Sciences in Kazan, the capital of the Republic of Tatarstan for hosting the conference and to the President of the Republic, H. E. Mintimer Sh. Shaimiyev who received the participants at the presidential palace in the Kazan Kremlin and who, without hesitation, agreed to write a Foreword for this volume.

I would wish also to express my personal indebtedness to Professor Aleksei Vasiliev and his colleagues in Moscow and Kazan who made the conference such a memorable event, and without whom we would not have had the Russian and Tatar papers both written and translated.

The papers were typed by Beverley Stubbs in Birmingham. I am deeply indebted to Hadi Enayat for his skill in editing the papers into a their present form, especially those which have been translated from Russian - only he and I know how much work is involved in this kind of enterprise.

Notes on the Contributors

R. M. Amirkhanov, Academy of Sciences of Tatarstan, Kazan, Tatarstan, Russian Federation.

R. Baltanov, Kazan Medical Institute, Tatarstan, Russian Federation.

G. Baltanova, Kazan Technological University, Tatarstan, Russian Federation.

P. Clark, Department of Theology, King's College, University of London, United Kingdom.

G. Krämer, Department of Middle Eastern Studies, University of Bonn, Germany.

A. Malashenko, Institute of Oriental Studies, Russian Academy of Sciences, Moscow, Russian Federation.

A. Moseyko, Centre for Civilizational Studies, Institute for African Studies, Russian Academy of Sciences, Moscow, Russian Federation.

J. S. Nielsen, Centre for the Study of Islam and Christian–Muslim Relations, Selly Oak Colleges, Birmingham, United Kingdom.

M. Sh. Shaimiev, President, Republic of Tatarstan, Russian Federation.

A. Vassiliev, Institute for African Studies, Russian Academy of Sciences, Moscow, Russian Federation.

V. M. Viktorin, Department of National Relations, attached to the Administration of the Astrakhan Region, Astrakhan, Russian Federation.

J. Waardenburg, Department of Theology, University of Lausanne, Switzerland.

THE CHRISTIAN–MUSLIM FRONTIER

Introduction

Jørgen S. Nielsen

Recent years have witnessed much talk of a 'clash of civilisations' between the Muslim world and Christendom, most of it superficial or ignorant and media-driven. There is little doubt that the cold war division of Europe distracted attention from complex relationships and local situations whose origins lie much further back than the establishment of the Soviet system out of the traumas of the first world war. But the Soviet system had itself, especially during the period of Stalin, exploited old identities when it suited and thus exacerbated their potential for conflict.

It should therefore come as no surprise that with the fall of the Soviet system, those older identities and relationships should again become visible. European Russia was, even before it expanded into Muslim Central Asia, a state which brought together ethnic and national groups for whom religion played an essential role in their self-understanding - and the religion was usually Christianity, in its Orthodox form, or Islam. When these histories reemerged into the public consciousness they coincidentally did so at a time when the outside world had become increasingly aware of possible differences of outlook between the Muslim world and Christendom generally.

This new awareness had come about as a result of a complex of developments: the increased politicisation of Islam especially following the Iranian revolution in 1979, the rise of Islamic opposition groups in countries like Algeria and Egypt, the growing appeal to *jihad* by militant groups in Lebanon and Afghanistan, the phenomenon of Islamic 'fundamentalism' and perceptions of Muslim terrorism. But the developments were not restricted to the Middle East: in western Europe immigrant communities and their growing numbers of adult offspring had increasingly been organising themselves on religious bases. Mosques were appearing in growing numbers in European cities, and Muslim organisations were asserting their right to participate in civic and political life. This culminated symbolically in the 'Rushdie' and 'headscarf' affairs in Britain and France respectively in 1989.

In such circumstances it was tempting in certain quarters, especially in the United States, to identify a new threat in the Muslim world which was lurking ready to replace that of communism. Clearly there were groups in eastern Europe who sought to exploit such perceptions for their own narrow interests, as we saw in the Serb propaganda leading into the post-Yugoslav conflicts as well as in some of the voices of extreme nationalism both in western Europe and in Russia.

Historically speaking there is little doubt that it is possible to identify a zone of interaction and flux between Muslim and Christian from the Mediterranean, through the Balkans and the Black Sea regions and north-eastward into the Volga basin. Geographically speaking it was never a zone which was easy to define or delimit; it was certainly a much wider zone than some recent popular analyses have tried to depict. It also extends beyond the immediately identifiable zone: Christian communities in the Arab world, especially in Egypt and the fertile crescent, have for centuries lived in everyday proximity with Muslims and at the same time have had on occasion to live with the attempts of outsiders to drag them into confrontation. More recently, Muslim communities have made their homes in the cities of western Europe where they too find themselves on occasion dragged into wider events beyond their control. As a result, in both cases, the majority communities and their leaders feel they have cause to look at the minorities with some degree of distrust.

But what is the nature of the interaction which takes place on this metaphorical Christian-Muslim frontier? Attempting to find some of the answers to this question was the motivation for holding a conference on the theme 'The Christian-Muslim frontier: History, myths and current perceptions' at the end of October 1993. The conference was organised jointly by the Institute for African Studies at the Russian Academy of Sciences in Moscow and the Centre for the Study of Islam and Christian-Muslim Relations (CSIC), Selly Oak Colleges, Birmingham.

The location of the conference coincided with the wider considerations of the subject to determine that the majority of the papers should concentrate on aspects of the question in relation to European Russia, especially as they are played out in Tatarstan and the Caucasus. To place this in a wider context papers were included to outline the historical precedents and resources for relations between Islam and Christendom, as well as studies of related interest dealing with Egypt and western Europe.

The conference took place in a context of political and intellectual excitement among our Tatar colleagues, as the republic sought to assert its sovereign status and Tatars were seizing the opportunity of recent liberalisation to explore their Tatar identity. But there was also great awareness of the dangers of pushing an exclusive nationalism too far, as they saw what was happening in the Caucasus and former Yugoslavia.

Taken together the papers indicate that such caution is well justified. A simplistic analysis is invariably wrong, and the perceptions of the interests of individual groups of people are seldom based primarily on religious identity. Economic and local interests can often bridge religious differences, and religious differences almost inevitably are activated at a secondary stage as a means to mobilise wider groups who do not necessarily otherwise share a perception of common interests. Such processes are particularly dangerous in a region where the principles of the respective religions are known only superficially and in a slogan-like form: generations of atheist propaganda and secularisation have marginalised or disposed completely of traditions of religious learning which could provide a source of continuous critique.

I

Encounters Between European Civilisation and Islam in History

Jacques Waardenburg

Any historian or sociologist of religion will recognise here a field of problems that has existed from the time of Muhammad onwards: what is the relationship between societies in which either Islam or Christianity are the dominant religion? What kind of interaction can take place between adherents of the Islamic faith and adherents of the Christian faith? Are we faced with a situation of intractable conflict, or are there possibilities of peaceful coexistence between adherents of the two faiths?

My contribution to this discussion will mainly deal with the historical dimension of the problem, but I will present some ideas of my own at the end. As far as history is concerned, I have always been fascinated by the encounters between Europe and the rest of the world, and in particular the interaction since the 14th century between European peoples and the Muslims who have lived on their borders. Europe suffered invasions by Arabs and Berbers from the south in the 8th and 9th centuries, by Tatar Mongols from the East in the 13th century, and by the Ottoman Turks in south-eastern Europe in the 14th and 15th centuries. Those regions of Europe which were invaded went on the defensive in order to survive; the widespread perception of the danger of Islam as an aggressor goes back to the traumatic experiences of this period.

Conquista and Reconquista of Europe

In a number of cases, it was largely in response to the conquests made by surrounding peoples who happened to be Muslims that Europeans went over to a counter-attack. This began with the expeditions of Charlemagne in southern France and north-east Spain, in 777–8, and the pushing back of the Arabs from mainland Italy by the beginning of the 11th century. The counter-attack took on larger proportions when Christians from the north began to reconquer the whole of Spain. This led to the ideology of the Reconquista and to military successes, starting with the capture of Toledo in 1085. The Catholic kings' offensive against the remaining Muslim states in Spain culminating with the fall of Grenada in 1492, and finally against any Muslim and Jewish presence in the country, was rounded off by the forced conversion of Muslims who had remained in Spain to Christianity and the expulsion of the 'Moriscos' from Spain in 1609.

In 1091 Sicily had been reconquered by the Normans, but here the Muslims stayed under the protection of the Norman kings, until their expulsion from the island in 1300. Indeed for several centuries both Spain and Sicily enjoyed peaceful coexistence between Muslims and Christians (in Moorish Spain there was also a thriving Jewish community). In Sicily it was the Christian Norman dynasty which encouraged coexistence, while in Spain peaceful relations between the communities are associated with Muslim rule.

There was more at stake than a simple Reconquista in the ill-fated venture of the Crusades in Syria and Palestine, where a Frankish presence lasted for nearly two centuries (1097–1291). As in Spain, here too there were strong ideological overtones and the Church played a leading role in both cases. The first Crusade in particular had strong religious motivations and eschatological features. Here it was the objective to possess the Holy Places which implied a struggle against Islam which came to be seen, as in Spain, as the arch-enemy of Christianity. The same ideology existed in the Byzantine empire before and after the Islamised Seljuq Turks invaded Anatolia, after the battle of Manzikert in 1071, where the imperial army was defeated. It would seem, however, that Orthodox Christianity, before and after the Great Schism of 1053, waged a less centralised and organised ideological warfare against Islam than Latin Christianity, whose Popes since Gregory VII (1073–1085) were for two centuries at the summit of their political and spiritual power in history, and where the various orders could be used besides the regular clergy to implement papal policies with regard to Muslims and Islam.

The Lithuanian capture of Kiev in 1370 and the Muscovites first military successes against the Tatars in 1380 led to the conquest and subjection of more and more territories once held by the Golden Horde and marked the beginning of a counter-offensive in eastern Europe comparable to the Reconquista in Spain. During the 15th century the Muscovite Grand Princes increased their power to the detriment of the Tatars and captured Novgorod in 1478. The Golden Horde in the meantime had been broken up into separate khanates. One of them, Kazan, was conquered by the Russians in 1552 bringing important territories of the Volga Tatars under their sway; Astrakhan fell in 1554. A West Siberian Khanate ceased to exist in 1584. Unlike their co-religionists in Spain and Italy, the Turkish Muslims did not generally leave the conquered areas.

Here it was not Roman Catholic but Russian Orthodox Christianity that provided the religious zeal, first for the reconquering of ancient Slav regions, then for intense proselytising activities while supporting the repressive policies of the tsars towards the Muslim Tatars in the conquered territories. This did not exclude that the Russians adopted many elements of Tatar culture, for instance in court ceremonial. Russian Orthodoxy later inspired the conquest of large Muslim regions outside Russia where Russian immigrants settled as they had in the reconquered Tatar regions. After Kazan and Astrakhan (16th century), successively Kazakhstan (17th century), the Crimea and the Caucasus (18th century), Transcaucasia and Turkestan (19th century) were brought under the sovereignty of the Tsars in what may be called an early imperial and colonial policy. By contrast with the situation in Spain and Italy in the medieval period, the inhabitants of the conquered Muslim territories could retain their religion and under Catherine II the Great (1762–96) toleration of Islam was officially proclaimed and its organisation under a Spiritual Directorate in Ufa established in 1784.

The third great counter-offensive or reconquest, after those in south-western and eastern Europe, was undertaken in south-eastern Europe, first by the Austrian Empire, later joined by Russia. Here the arch-enemy was the Ottoman Empire. From Mehmet II's conquest of Constantinople in 1453 until the peace of Karlowitz, where the Ottomans had to recognise their first defeat and abandon Hungary (1699), the empire was viewed as the most formidable danger to Europe. Austria's reconquest, in which Hungary later co-operated, was strongly backed by Catholic ideology and put the possibilities offered by the printing press for a new kind of propaganda to good use. If one may speak of contempt in the case of Russian Orthodox anti-Islamic ideology, Catholic anti-Islamic ideology betrayed a much deeper kind of hatred. The two sieges of Vienna, in 1529 and 1683, though unsuccessful, may be in part responsible for this harsher attitude. Another reason may have been (after a first period of relative tolerance) the sometimes bitter fate of Christians living under Ottoman oppression in some regions of the Balkans. Consequently the Austrian reconquest could be viewed as a war of liberation.

The 19th century saw the emergence of a new force: the birth of nationalism leading to insurrections of Christian peoples, not only for the sake of religion but for the sake of nationhood. The Greek war of independence (1821–30) is an example of such a struggle as are the wars for the restoration of Serbia and the freedom of the other Balkan peoples. The last of these states to declare independence from the Ottomans were Bulgaria in 1908, followed by Albania in 1912. The Russians were instrumental in helping their Slav brethren against the Turks. With the Treaty of Bucharest in 1913 and that of Lausanne in 1923, Turkey only kept a small fraction of its former European Rumelia and the reconquest of Europe from Islam was finished. The Muslim presence in Europe was confined to small, powerless communities scattered across Albania, Yugoslavia and Russia in particular.

This was, however, to be only part of the story. Europeans encountered Muslims far beyond Europe's frontiers. I have already mentioned the Russian occupation of Kazakhstan, Transcaucasia and Turkestan. In fact, as early as the 16th century economically attractive areas of Africa and Asia witnessed the establishing of Portuguese, Dutch, British and French commercial posts in coastal regions, many of which were inhabited by Muslims. From the end of the eighteenth century European ambitions grew. In the 1760s Britain established political authority, via the East India Company, in Bengal and subsequently extended it throughout the Indian subcontinent. It occupied strategic posts on the main sea routes. France tried to establish itself in Egypt in 1798 but failed; its colonial adventures started with the invasion of Algeria in 1830. Holland gained control of what is today Indonesia. Looking at the world map of the 1920's one is amazed to see that nearly the whole Muslim world at the time was under European political control. The only Muslim countries which escaped occupation were Turkey, Iran, Afghanistan, Saudi Arabia and Yemen.

We may call the period from the end of the 18th till the middle of the 20th century an age of European imperialism and colonisation of Muslim territories. It carried with it something of a revenge against the Islam which at the time had nearly been driven out of Europe, but which had earlier represented a major military, political and ideological danger to the continent. As far as I can see few Europeans had a positive view of Islam and the fact that a number of insurrections against the European colonial administration used Islam as their slogan cast it in the role of the great disrupter of the world order established by Europe until 1939, and by North America and Europe together from 1945 onwards.

On an even larger scale, a political confrontation with the intangible enemy called 'Islam' continued throughout the conflicts around the state of Israel in the Middle East, throughout the Cold War and the strategic encirclement of the southern regions of the Soviet Union, throughout the efforts to guarantee Western oil supplies, and throughout the extension of Western protection to the state of Israel. Furthermore the rise of Islamic movements all over the Muslim world, in particular in the regions surrounding Europe has reignited feelings of animosity towards Islam even though these countries no longer pose a serious political or military threat. Studying history is useful because it throws light on the extent to which the current conflict between Europe and Islam continues to be marked by the traumas of the past when Europe needed Islam as its antagonist.

Religious Imagination and Ideology Hostile to Islam

Only certain parts of Europe suffered the invasions of Muslim peoples from the south, the east and the south-east. Regions like Scandinavia, the British Isles, Germany, the Benelux region and the northern part of France had no direct experience of Muslims. Only a small number of people who went to Muslim regions acquired this experience: those who participated in the Crusades or engaged in commerce. To them can be added, since the middle of the 19th century, the great number of those who carried out military or administrative duties in the colonies, settled in Muslim countries, worked there as Christian missionaries, perhaps in hospitals or schools, or simply went there in order to start a new life or to have adventure.

Yet all over Europe a rich store of images developed around Islam;

and several studies have been devoted to the subject during the last decades. Many of these images connected with Islam were themselves of a religious nature, like ideas about the person of Muhammad, his claim to prophethood, and the claim that the Qur'an is God's word. These religious notions were not without perversion such as the depiction of Islam as a Satanic religion.

These religious ideas could be channelled into religious ideology, establishing an absolute opposition between the Christian world with its thoroughly good religion and the Muslim world with an evil religion which aimed to destroy Christianity. The existing conflict could not but enhance the idea that Islam and Christianity were each other's absolute opposites. Fighting Muslims was not only necessary in self-defence; it also became a kind of holy war, a terrible war because the truth slowly emerged that it was impossible to defeat this enemy by force of arms.

In this connection the religious hope, throughout the Middle Ages, that behind this Islam threatening Europe there was somewhere a Christian kingdom, linked to the name of Prester John, is significant. If only the Christians of Europe could get in touch with their hidden brethren behind the Muslim territories, and if the Christians could attack these territories from both sides at the same time, the terrible enemy might finally be defeated for good! Such an imagination testifies to the frightful fear in which the European Christians lived, in particular with the advance of the Seljuks in Anatolia, of Saladin and his successors on the Levant, and of the Ottoman Turks crossing the Dardanelles.

That religious images could be channelled into religious ideology and put to serve war becomes evident in the ideology of the Reconquista and the subsequent 'religious cleansing' of Spain and Portugal with the expulsion of Jews and Muslims by the Catholic kings. We see this also in the religious propaganda materials used in the Austrian war effort against the Ottoman Turks. The same could be said for the Orthodox mobilisation of Greeks, Serbs, Bulgars and other Balkan peoples in the wars of independence against the Ottoman empire. It was not only against the empire or against the Turkish soldiers that the battle had to be waged: it was directed, finally, against Islam, a force of evil that had to be subdued. As far as I can discover, a similar note was struck in the Russian conquests in the Crimea, the Caucasus and Central Asia: the Christian state should dominate Islam.

... was alive in certain circles when the ... ...d in their colonial venture in Muslim ... ... carried out at the instigation of the ... ... research about Vatican policies may shed ... ...s interests in the colonial venture. Missionary ... ...considered the latter as a welcome opportunity to ... ...ospel, to assist local Christian communities living under ... ...up, to establish medical care, schools and social help for people ... ...spective of their faith. Christian politicians might press their governments to give more support to the Christian missions in the colonies, but the missionaries themselves had sometimes a very critical attitude to the way in which colonial policies were carried out.

On a more spiritual level, missionaries, who often felt a great dedication and love for the Muslims with whom they worked, had a sombre idea of Islam, although it could be mitigated by better education. Since it was their vocation and task to spread the Gospel, anything which stood in their way could not but be bad. This was held to be the case with Islam which, in their view, dominated Muslims' minds, individually and socially, making them impenetrable to the Christian message. In other words, on a spiritual level too, a mythical view of an evil entity, Islam, directly opposed to the good entity in which the Christians believed. This obscured the obvious truth that it was a whole range of hard economic, social and political factors, rather than Islam which had placed Muslims as well as others at the mercy of the European powers. Such factors prevented new interpretations of Islam. They also made it impossible for Muslims to leave Islam altogether. The very assignment the missionaries had accepted, to work for proselytism in the sense of replacing the entity Islam by the entity Christianity, led them to perceive Islam as an obnoxious, dominating system standing in the way of Christianity as they imagined it. In fact, this too was a mythical view of Islam and prevented the missionaries from enquiring about the realities of Muslim societies. These missionaries showed little scholarly interest.

Summarising, we must conclude that, because of the fact that not only the Islamic faith and religion but also Muslim societies and cultures were badly known at the time, imagination imposed itself on reality. This imagination could be made into and used as an ideology with its own mythical view of reality. According to this view, there was a monolithic entity 'Islam'. This entity had threatened Europe and Christianity. The time had come to free the world from this danger, to push it back, to dominate it, to eliminate it. The great majority of European Christians saw Islam as an evil monolithic religious entity which held Muslim societies and individuals under its sway and which ought not to exist. This was what I would call a religious mythical view of Islam, the consequences of which are still quite palpable in Christian circles today. We shall now see that such a mythical view was, and still is, also held in non-religious circles.

Some Non-religious Attitudes Towards Islam

What is to be said about the non-religious ideas of Europe about Islam? If we leave aside the powerful political ideologies that were at the basis of the European colonial expansion, we may briefly consider three trends of imagination which turned into ideology and had important consequences both for the ways in which Europeans looked at Islam and for the ways in which a Western-oriented cultural elite in Muslim countries received European social and cultural thought. Europe (and the United States) not only had their religious missionaries; throughout the 19th and 20th centuries there had been a drive to export the values which had been nurtured there to the rest of the world, primarily to the neighbouring Muslim regions and countries, if only to give them education. During the second half of the nineteenth, and the first half of the twentieth century, not only Muslims living in Europe but also a Western-oriented cultural elite in Muslim countries were remarkably receptive to these values. Further study is needed in order to determine which elements of European culture were received, according to various cultural milieus and social groups and according to the humanistic, Protestant, Catholic or Orthodox orientations with which Muslims came into contact.

The first source of new values of a non-religious nature, for which the Enlightenment prepared the way, was the French Revolution of 1789 and the ideals proclaimed by it. These ideas found acceptance in particular among bourgeois European emancipatory movements, and then among a younger Muslim emancipatory elite preparing to engage in the modernisation of the various Muslim countries: Young Ottomans and Young Turks, Egyptians and North Africans, Syrians and Iranians, Muslim Indians and Indonesians were all influenced by these ideas. The values proclaimed by the French revolution had an especially strong appeal among a Muslim bourgeois elite oriented toward France. French colonial and foreign policy aptly developed the ideology of France's *mission civilisatrice*. It had the same mythical view of Islam as the religious ideologies, except that Islam was seen as an obstacle in the first place to European civilisation and its blessings, rather than to the Christian religion. Muslim peoples needed to be educated and it is quite touching to see how much effort the Europeans devoted to this task. Islam was also tragically misunderstood by those who had no religious faith themselves and did their best to emancipate Muslims from their religion, that is to say to marginalise, if not to suppress, Islam culturally. One of the effects of this policy of a *mission civilisatrice* was that a certain French speaking cultural elite in North Africa, the Middle East and French sub-Saharan Africa assimilated the prevailing French outlook on many things including Islam. In a qualified form these ideals predominated among the French speaking leadership in certain Muslim countries until the 1970s. In this perspective Islam as a faith and religion was simply marginalised or subordinated to the values of liberal modernity.

As far as I can see, Muslims who were educated according to the British system with its way of life and values were bound to Britain, whereas those who had received a Russian education were bound to Russia. Later, of course, a reaction against this Western 'cultural colonisation' made itself felt, but at least during colonial times this Westernised Muslim elite constituted a bridge between Europe and the Muslim countries. The educated European public who were informed about Islam by these Muslim intellectuals did develop sympathies with Islam as long as it could be seen to embrace modern liberal values similar to those accepted in educated Western circles. In other words, Western images of Islam could be remedied by recognising in Muslims values that were accepted in the West.

Another source of non-religious imagination was the socialist movement born in Europe in the first half of the nineteenth century, with its fight for human dignity and justice, its opposition to colonialism and its appreciation of struggles for emancipation and freedom, including the fight for the national independence. The Russian revolutions of 1917 and in particular the ideals proclaimed by the leaders of the October revolution had a profound impact not only among European socialists but also among certain groups of Muslims who saw in them a path to liberation. Within Europe these ideals were at first considered as the realisation of values proclaimed by the socialist movement since its conception.

They also found acceptance among socialist individuals and groups more oriented towards revolution in the colonies, including Muslim countries, albeit to a limited extent because of the anti-religious posture of the movement. In the socialist view, Muslims should be educated to understand the real forces of history and to change their often passive history through revolutionary action. Needless to say, this idea of educating the Muslims differed fundamentally not only from the educational ideas of the missionaries but also from the bourgeois education which had lost the revolutionary impetus of the French Revolution. The socialist and then communist ideals, however, had an appeal for a new generation fighting not only for national independence but also for a new kind of society. Soviet foreign policy used the socialist and communist ideals in order to bind the various socialist and communist movements to the Soviet Union, claiming to promote a world revolution in the name of Marxism–Leninism. This linkage was made all the more successful because of the organisation of an international network of communist political parties radically subservient to the authorities in Moscow. Only a critical mind could see that the socialist ideals had been perverted through being incorporated into a power structure, something which until then was only known to have happened in certain religious organisations and churches.

It is important to realise that the political leadership in nearly all Muslim countries after independence sought at most a socialist kind of political system which was not anti-religious, that is to say against Islam. Notwithstanding the fact that, with the exception of Albania, no Muslim country modelled itself completely on the Soviet Union, socialist ideals, partly rediscovered in the Qur'an and the religious tradition, became accepted in a number of Muslim countries. This gave their governments a certain credit among socialist modernists. European socialists, however, could sympathise with those forms of Muslim socialism in which they recognised values held by themselves.

A third strand of cultural orientation in Europe was more rational than the two just described, which were in one way or another linked with the European revolutions. This was secular rationalism and empiricism, which inspired the ideologies of secularism (*laïcité*) and positivism. This approach allowed for the development of scholarly research with regard to Muslim societies on a pragmatic basis, as carried out in the *tanzimat* reforms of the Ottoman empire and the modernisation policy of Mehmet Ali in Egypt. Such modernisation efforts were promoted by the colonial administrations and then by the nationalist leaders who were forced to subject their new nations to the economic and social development necessary for their survival. Needless to say, the leaders concerned had to take into account basic Islamic values that ought not to be infringed. Islam, in this view, had to be split. Its eternal religious duties and truths were to be respected, whereas its legal prescriptions and local customs had to be adapted to the demands of modernity. It should be noted that this trend too led to ideology; many Europeans saw economic and social development as the right future for Muslim countries, just as many Muslim intellectuals saw this as the path to the future.

Many Europeans looked at Muslim countries basically as developing countries and sympathised with the Muslim elite engaging in development. To the extent that certain Islamic values could be mobilised for such active development work, Islam was seen as a more positive force than before. Development was the common enterprise of Europeans (Westerners) and Muslims alike. It was forgotten, however, that European models of modernisation and development could not be implemented in Muslim countries as they had been in Europe and went against certain basic Islamic norms and values. Like the missionaries, liberals and socialists, the modernisers used Western models and exported Western values that were not practicable and not acceptable for Muslims, who had to develop their own models and put their own values into practice.

These three ideological trends born in Europe seem to have been the most important expressions of non-religious imagination and thought, and they had a certain impact not only on nineteenth and twentieth century European views of Islam but also on the thinking of the Westernised Muslim elites. Like the religious imagination, the non-religious images and ideas about Islam were a product of European civilisation. These ideas, as well as the ideologies resulting from them, whatever their virtues, had after all an ethnocentric character and could too easily be used to dominate Muslim peoples, or at least be accused of being used as such. Moreover, they had no means to understand Islam as a religion in general.

Positive Interaction Between Europe and Islam

In the foregoing we stressed the role of power and imagination in the relations between European civilisation and Islam throughout history. We paid more attention to European perceptions and actions concerning Muslims and Islam than to Muslim perceptions and actions concerning Europeans and Christianity. It should indeed readily be admitted that this same history also testifies to positive encounters and collaboration between Europeans and Muslims, direct contacts which did not result in negative stereotypes of the other and outright celebration of the self.

There were instances of positive attitudes and cultural exchanges in 10th to 11th-century Spain, 11th to 12th-century Sicily, 12th-century Syria and Palestine. Leaving the commercial contact with Mamluk Syria and Egypt and the various provinces of the Ottoman Empire aside, we must acknowledge creative cultural and exchanges in Cairo and Alexandria, St. Petersburg and Kazan, Lahore and Delhi in the later nineteenth and early twentieth centuries. There were continuous trade links in which Tatars, Syrians and Lebanese, Egyptian and other Muslim traders in Asia and Africa played a key role. In the field of thought, literature, art and music certain creations of European and Muslim regions were able to cross political frontiers and certain ideological barriers. In the field of science and education, technology and research there was and is an increasing co-operation between Europeans and Muslims working at European institutions. Communications technology and media offer possibilities of positive co-operation to further understanding between Muslims outside and inside Europe on the one hand, and Europeans outside and inside Muslim countries on the other.

Some Conclusions From the Past

Looking back at the history of the encounters between European civilisation and Islam, some conclusions may be drawn which may throw light on future prospects. I would like to mention five points.

First, the notion of European civilisation is an ambiguous one, covering both summits of genius and creativity and the worst excesses of destruction and oppression both inside and outside Europe. The three Great Wars, including the 'cold' war, which this continent had known during the twentieth century, were utterly self-destructive and brought about a definite break with the civilisation which existed in this continent before 1914. Over against the forces working toward Europe's gradual unification, there are also dangerous and divisive forces at work in south-eastern and eastern Europe. The frightful separation of western and eastern Europe which lasted more then forty years has not been overcome yet, and in both parts considerable Muslim minorities are living with hopes of emancipation and equal partnership in the European house.

Yet certain values and institutions appear to have struck deep roots. Multi-party democracy and respect for human rights have been established in most European countries. In the field of culture there is an incredible variety of expression, a large number of independent cultural institutions, and a high value is placed on the individual, reason and critical judgment. Here and there we find a recognition of mistakes made in the past, including the lust for domination, chauvinism and self-aggrandisement, as well as a mystification or mythical view of Europe. As a consequence a certain reserve is to be noted with regard to religion as well as a certain critical attitude to the present state of European societies and the people constituting them, both Christians and Muslims

Second, the realities of Islam, like those of Europe, are more complicated than earlier generations were able to realise. Although oversimplified and distorted images of Islam are still common, we are now able to see its religious and ideological variations in relation to historical and social conditions. Like Europe, Islam is an entity which takes many different forms, to be studied in relation to the societies in which they occur. Behind current European views we have been able to perceive some basic mythical views of Islam as Europe's great antagonist, representing an evil force in opposition to the expansion of an essentially good Europe and pure Christian religion.

Muslim societies have their own values. In social organisation the natural units of tribe, clan and family play an important role; the concentration of power enjoys religious legitimation; social institutions and office holders equally receive a kind of transcendent respect. In the cultural field Muslim expressions testify to an extraordinary sensitivity to harmony, much attention being given to inter-subjective realities and much value attached to matters of honour and justice where both the group and the individual are concerned. In contrast to

Europe, Muslim societies are anything but reserved about religion, Islam being absolutised and presented as a religion providing answers to all the problems of mankind. After a period in which a Westernised Muslim elite sustained rather liberal and even universalistic views of the different religions of mankind, we now witness an increasing particularism among Islamic groups and institutions.

Third, the past shows the dangers of a certain Eurocentrism, leading to an unrealistic assessment of Europe's place in the world at large, or a certain blindness to the internal contradictions and tensions in European societies which continue to challenge basic human values. Similarly the past shows the danger of Islamocentrism, leading to an unrealistic assessment of Islam's place in the world at large. At the present time there is an ongoing struggle for the recognition of pluralism within and outside Muslim communities, exacerbated by the weakness of democratic procedures and institutions in many Muslim countries. Societies anywhere in the world continuously enduring economic and political hardships are exposed to the dangers of ideological and political extremism.

Fourth, any critical reflection will recognise the negative consequences of European isolationism with regard to the surrounding Muslim peoples which often have been perceived as barbarian, uncivilised, undeveloped or immature in male–female relationships. It will also see the negative effects of some fatal conflicts of recent years in which, both in reality and in imagination, old Christian–Muslim conflicts were revived: the wars in Lebanon, the second Gulf War, the wars in and around Bosnia, the Armenia–Azerbaijan conflict. Even if it is recognised that these have not been wars of religion, there is no doubt that Muslims have felt Europeans to be their potential or real enemy and tended to act accordingly. The relationships between Europe and its neighbouring countries may be threatened less by wars of religion than by the rise of ethnic nationalism of various kinds, the revolt of the poor against the rich, and the persistent tendency not to forget the past. Both within and around Europe there are peoples, including Israelis and Palestinians, who are still in the grip of past sufferings.

Fifth, a final conclusion from historical work is that in a number of cases ancient structures and traditions, sometimes reaching back centuries, are in the process of change or simply breaking down. People take different attitudes to this fact and in this way have an important influence on the future. Some embrace the risks of change while others grasp on to the certainties of tradition. This holds true for the attitudes of Europeans particularly European Christians towards Muslims and vice versa. Fundamentally, all of this is a matter of choice of a certain, or rather, an uncertain future. Three questions appear to be inescapable:

(i) What does Europe think of its surrounding Muslim peoples and countries and what do these peoples and countries think of Europe?
(ii) How should relations between European and Muslim countries, societies and persons be regulated in terms of institutions, ideas and values when tensions arise?
(iii) What resources exist in Europe to deal with present-day and future challenges to Christian–Muslim 'frontiers' and the idea of Islam as 'the new enemy'? And what resources exist in the neighbouring Muslim countries to deal with the same challenges of a Muslim–Christian 'frontier' and the idea of Europe as 'the rich enemy'?

And the Christians?

It would seem that certain traditional attitudes of Christian churches with regard to Islam are in process of revision and change.

(i) At the Second Vatican Council (1962–65) the Roman Catholic Church seems to have abandoned its old policy of seeking to dominate Islam with the help of worldly powers, announcing instead its desire to open dialogue with Muslims and Islam. As far as I can see, the most interesting intellectual and spiritual explorations as to Christian–Muslims relations have taken place here. On a practical level, since the Second Vatican Council an immense effort had been made, even on the local level, to give Christians much better instruction about the tenets of the Islamic faith and practice and to encourage peaceful coexistence and dialogue with Muslim neighbours, such as Muslim immigrants in Europe. Because of its age-long presence in Muslim countries and its accumulation of knowledge through theologically trained specialists, the Roman Catholic Church has at present a place of honour with regard to Christian–Muslim relationships.
(ii) In the various Protestant Churches two different lines are clearly

distinguishable. On the one hand there are those often called evangelicals, proposing straightforward proselytism among Muslims in the old missionary tradition. On the other hand there are those who desperately are looking for new ways for Christians and Muslims to live together.

Following the social line, the World Council of Churches have been organising for some twenty years or more what may be called 'experimental' encounters between Christians and Muslims, to which Roman Catholics have been invited too. Such encounters have taken place both on a higher level between chosen representatives of the two religions and on an ordinary level between Christians and Muslims living in the same region. In contrast to the Catholic approach, the World Council of Churches had appealed much less to specialists in Islamic studies or social scientists and has attached less value to institutional representation. Both the Catholic and Protestant approaches to Islam have undergone changes due to decolonisation and the construction of new viable countries and societies in the Third World.

(iii) The Orthodox Churches in the Middle East have maintained an open attitude to Muslims and Islam and have practised dialogue when possible, in particular during the last thirty years or so. The Orthodox Churches in Greece and the Balkan countries have maintained a defensive attitude with regard to anything that has to do with Turkey, Muslims and Islam. The community with the 'mythical view' of Islam, as described above, is unmistakable here.

The Russian Orthodox Church, allied before 1917 to the Tsarist state which kept the policy of domination of its Muslim subjects, has during the last 75 years been forced to revise its role in society, a society held until recently to be one without religion. No new theological views seem to have been developed with regard to Islam. In practice Orthodox Christians and Muslims in the old USSR can work together, on condition that religion not be discussed.

A practical question is whether the Russian Orthodox Church has specialists who know Islam well and whether they have any contacts with Muslim religious leaderships. A broader question is whether the Church has developed new views about Islam and Muslims inside and outside Russia since the end of the communist regime. What are the attitudes of Russian Orthodox Christians today towards Muslim peoples inside and outside Russia?

I would like to end this paper by mentioning three elements which are nearly always present in present-day Christian thinking about Islam and which, in my opinion, indicate to what extent Christians in Europe are still paying tribute to the past and having difficulty in becoming clear-minded about the future:

Firstly, many Christians in Europe are not able to see that their attitudes towards Muslims and Islam go back to political structures which are definitely outdated. For instance they see 'Islam' as a monolithic entity (the 'mythical' view referred to above) and they associate the idea of war, struggle and animosity with it, as if they need an enemy for their own sake. Or they make an intrinsic connection between a certain people and a certain religion without admitting plurality or even real diversity. This leads to a similar kind of 'mythical' view demanding unconditional loyalty from all persons whatever their personal faith, conviction or ideas.

Secondly, many Christians in Europe are not able to think or speak of Islam without feeling some need to exert power. They associate Islam with power and they respond by thinking of their own power and how to increase it. In other words, their discourse about Islam has to do with power rather than with faith or religion. It is like reflexes from ancient times: feeling threatened by Islam or feeling the need to dominate Islam. In fact we have to deal again with a 'mythical' view of a powerful and threatening Islam.

Thirdly, many Christians in Europe are still not capable of thinking rationally and empirically about Muslims and Islam. They are unable to distinguish between facts and interpretations, cause and effect. They seem to be blinded by mythical views and mystifications presented by their own authorities as well as Muslims tending to mystify the Islam in which they believe. The media, attitudes of negotiation and various emotions also prevent Christians from thinking about Muslims and Islam as something alive, as an acceptable alternative. Is it inability or unwillingness which prevents so many Christians in Europe from appreciating a way of life and ideas other than their own? These are questions which are relevant for our topic: where the simple recognition of the right of existence of someone different and the sincere wish for a better knowledge of that other person, society or religion are absent, any encounter risks becoming a conflict.

References

Abu-Lughod, Ibrahim, *The Arab Rediscovery of Europe. A study in cultural encounters.* Princeton: Princeton University Press, 1963.

Barthold, V. V., *La decouverte de l-Asie. Histoire de l'orientalisme en Europe et en Russie.* Paris: Payot, 1947.

Bennigsen, Alexandre & S. Enders Wimbush, *Muslims of the Soviet Empire. A Guide.* London: C. Hurst, 1985.

Bondarevsky, Grigori, *Muslims and the West.* New Delhi: Sterling Publishers, 1985.

Daniel Norman, *Islam and the West.* Edinburgh: Edinburgh University Press, 1960.

——*Islam, Europe and Empire.* Edinburgh: Edinburgh University Press, 1966.

——*The Arabs and Medieval Europe.* London: Longman & Beirut: Librairie du Liban, 1975.

Gabrieli, Francesco (Dir), *Histoire et civilisation de l'Islam en Europe. Arabes et Turks en Occident du VIIe au XXe siecle.* Paris: Bordas, 1983.

Hentsch, Thierry, *L'Orient imaginaire. La vision politique occidentale de l'Est mediterraneen.* Paris: Ed. Minuit, 1988.

Hitti, Philip, *Islam and the West. A historical cultural survey.* Princeton, NJ: Van Nostrand, 1962.

Hourani, Albert, *Europe and the Middle East.* Berkeley & Los Angeles: University of California Press, 1980.

Kratchkovsky, I. Y., *Among Arabic Manuscripts. Memories of libraries and men.* Leiden: Brill, 1953.

——*Die russische Arabistik. Umrisse ihrer Entwicklung.* Leipzig: Harrassowitz, 1957.

Lewis, Archibald (ed.), *The Islamic World and the West, 622–1492, A.D.* New York: John Wiley, 1970.

Lewis, Bernard, *The Middle East and the West.* Bloomington, Ind.: Indiana University Press, 1964.

——*The Muslim Discovery of Europe.* New York & London: Norton, 1982.

Rodinson, Maxime, *Europe and the Mystique of Islam.* London: I. B. Tauris, 1987.

Said, Edward W., *Orientalism.* New York: Pantheon Books, 1978.

Semaan, Khalil I., *Islam and the Medieval West. Aspects of intercultural relations.* Albany, NY: SUNY Press, 1980.

Siebernich, Gereon & Hendrik Budde (Hrg.), *Europa und der Orient 800–1900.* Gutersloh & Munchen: Bertelsmann Lexikon Verlag, 1989.

Southern, R. W., *Western Views of Islam in the Middle Ages.* Cambridge, Mass.: Harvard University Press, 1962.

Waardenburg, J. J., *L'Islam dans le miroir de l'Occident.* Berlin: Mouton & Walther de Gruyter, 3rd ed. 1970.

Watt, W. Montgomery, *The Influence of Islam on Medieval Europe.* Edinburgh: Edinburgh University Press, 1972.

2

Russia's Destinies and Islam

Aleksei Vasiliev

The concepts 'civilisation', 'civilised conduct', 'joining the civilised world' sound unfortunate in the Russian political slang of today. The apologists of 'accustoming Russia to civilisation' behave as if there is no diversity of civilisations: Western Christian, Confucian, Muslim, Eastern Slavonic and so on. Each of them has a value of its own and will make a contribution to the global pluralist civilisation of the 21st century. The dominance of the West in the Far East is questioned even in the field of technology. Whereas this situation is not yet characteristic, say, of the Muslim world, who can predict the future?

But this discredited idea has not appeared in today's confused and diseased Russian socio-political thought by chance. It reflects the unsolved question of Russia's identity. After the collapse of Communism, an extremist radical form of ideology, imported from the West, the dispute between the 'Westernists' and 'Slavophiles' transformed into a dispute between the 'democrats' and 'etatists'. The former advocate the transplanting of Western values to inhospitable Russian soil, while the latter stress preservation or renaissance of Russia's special and exclusive features. Naturally, there are no hard and fast lines within the framework of socio-political struggle between different trends. Nor is there an organic connection between 'democratic' or 'etatists' convictions and their followers' attitude to the world of Islam and Russia's Muslim citizens. People who belong to opposite camps may close ranks, for different reasons, in their negative attitude to Islam. The pupils of the lowest class in the school of free market economics and democracy are trying arrogantly to teach Muslim countries and peoples 'the values of civilisation'; frantic chauvinists are imposing the idea of *'Russland über alles'* upon them. Yet, strangely enough, both 'Communist internationalists' and anti-

Communist 'new Eurasians' advocate understanding and cooperation with the world of Islam.

The picture is complicated by the play of history and geography that has placed Russia in a position between the West and the Muslims, whose relations are not yet harmonious.

The earlier confrontation between the West and the East and between Western democracy and Communism is being replaced by that between the West and the Islamic world. A partly real, but essentially artificial image of 'the enemy', personified by the Muslim world, is created in Western public opinion, while Russia is involved in an unnecessary and alien conflict with a potentially fatal outcome. The menace to Russia's destinies could manifest itself in three ways. Firstly, in her relations with the countries of the world of Islam beyond the former USSR, particularly with those which choose non-Western socio-political models. Following the West's political conduct, Russia may find herself in needless confrontation with these countries. Moscow's unfriendly attitude to Iran and Libya, which have not taken any anti-Russian actions is the best example of this. If this pro-Western stance is continued, it will lead inevitably to further weakening of Russia's position in the Muslim world.

However, some of the activities of Muslim states in Central Asia, Caucasia and in Russia herself are perceived in Moscow as hostile to its national interests. Such perceptions are an expression of nostalgia for the bipolar world throughout the Muslim world, of partial coincidence of the objective interests of Russia, a regional power (but no longer a superpower), and the Muslim countries in their relations with the West.

The menace may be even greater if Russia fails to arrange dialogue and cooperation with the post-Soviet Muslim states. It is not only a question of economic and strategic interests (Russia shares thousands of kilometres of common frontiers with these states). It is also a question of the destiny of the Russian and Russian speaking population in the former union republics. The spectre of Bosnia/Herzegovina is haunting Central Asia and Trans-Caucasia.

The third consideration is Russian society itself. A feature of Russia's historical development and geostrategic position is that she not only lived beside the Muslim world, but a part of it is situated within her. The interaction between the two civilisations has been a period both of struggle and of cultural, socio-political and anthropological exchange. Historically, the Russians are not only of Slavonic 'blood', but also Finno-Ugric and Turkic. There are common elements in music, dance, ornaments, poetry, ethnic character and psychology of the Russians and Turkic peoples. The traditions of collectivism rather than of individualism are characteristics both of the Orthodox Russians and of the Muslim Turks. The temporary success of the Communist experiment in Russia and the Muslim regions of the USSR was determined, *inter alia*, by the stress on group and collectivist values to the detriment of the individual and personal values. The economy and everyday life of Russian and Tatar villages in the Volga region differ only in minor details. The ranks of the Cossacks were continuously replenished by Kalmucks, Circassians, Tatars and Kazakhs. Hundreds of Russian noble families were of Turkic origin. Remote parallels to this situation may be found in Spain, the Balkans and India. But parallels are dangerous. The sentence of history eradicated in the Iberian Peninsula, leaving traces in culture and people's anthropological type and psychology. A bloody drama has flared up again in the Balkans. India is seeking the path of coexistence of Muslims and non-Muslims. Will she find them?

The percentage of Muslims in Russia and, say, France (including citizens, legal and illegal immigrants) is almost equal. But their roots differ: while the Muslims of the Western countries are newcomers, the Russian Muslims are indigenous inhabitants. Islam appeared on the banks of the Volga some decades before Rus was baptised in the waters of the Dnieper.

Islam and Orthodoxy interacted and fought, cooperated and quarrelled within the common continental space. As a whole, it was a process of mutual penetration and influence. Russian social anthropologist L. N. Gumilev was of the opinion that Ancient Rus and the Great Steppe formed a united ethnographic space at the beginning of the second millennium after Christ. Russia occupied a peculiar position between the East and the West. Russia herself formed first as a multiethnic and then as a multi-confessional country. Many contemporary scholars hold that some of her inhabitants, e.g., in the Volga-Ural region, given their linguistic, ethnic, religious and even racial diversity, have acquired common features and developed a common cultural stratum, way of life and style of behaviour. This did not prevent the emergence of elements of extreme nationalism among them, though.

After the annexation of Central Asia, the number of Muslims in Russia exceeded that in the Ottoman empire. The standards of respect for Islam and the Muslims' peculiar traditions developed in Russia gradually. The local elites were gradually incorporated into the all-Russian nobility and then the commercial and industrial elite.

The Tatars of Kazan and of the Volga region as a whole became a kind of cultural bridge between Russia and Central Asia. Dozens of thousands of Tatar merchants, businessmen, and intellectuals migrated to Central Asia.

The annexation of Central Asia to Russia was, on the one side, an act of colonial enslavement. On the other side, it resulted in the cessation of internecine wars, the abolition of slavery, a notable upsurge and transformation of the economy, the emergence of the working class and trader-entrepreneurs. The Central Asian peoples' choice during this historical period was not between independent development and submission to Russia, but between submission to China, Iran, Afghanistan or to Russia.

Perhaps this was the reason why Jadidism, the Muslim reformation movement which spread in the Muslim regions of Russia in the late 19th and early 20th centuries, was aimed at granting them religious and national autonomy within the framework of the Russian empire. Even the highly prestigious Ottoman empire did not become the main centre that attracted the Russian Muslims as a whole. This was characteristic even of the qadimists, the Muslim traditionalists, who opposed the Jadids.

After the revolution of 1917 the Soviet Union did its best to portray itself as a protector of Muslims' rights. One of the Bolsheviks' first steps was the publication of the Address to All Toiling Muslims of Russia and the East. Relying on their military strength, propaganda, demagogy and cooperation of such Muslim revolutionaries as Mullanur Vahitov, Nariman Narimanov, Fitrat, Faizullah Khojaev and Mirsaid Sultan-Galiev, Bolsheviks established their control over all Muslim regions of the former Russian empire. The Bolsheviks managed to enlist the support of some Muslim *ulama* in combating anti-Soviet guerillas. An example was a conference of *ulama* held in 1923 under the slogan 'Soviet power does not contradict the Shari'a'.

A characteristic example of compromise with Muslims in order to gain their support in the civil war was the decree of the government of the Turkestan autonomous republic, passed in the summer of 1921, when virtually the whole countryside was controlled by the Basmachi, anti-Soviet armed guerillas. *Waqf* properties were returned to mosques. Clergy were allowed to run primary schools, as they did before the revolution. Friday was proclaimed an official holiday. Shari'a courts were reopened and *Nahkamai Shari'a*, a religious directorate, was set up in Tashkent. These measures deprived the Basmachi of the very ideological weapon they relied on - the slogan of protection of Islam from godless Bolsheviks' persecution - and contributed to their final defeat.

However, when Stalin established himself in Russia, he came to the conclusion that there must be a single god (himself), a single 'religion' (atheism), a single culture (the 'Soviet socialist' culture), a single political organisation (the Bolshevik party, interlaced with the secret police) and a single form of ownership (collective ownership) in the country. Resistance of the feudal elites, conservative clergy and traditionalist-minded peasantry (insurrections in Northern Caucasia and the Basmachi movement) was suppressed. The independently thinking Muslim revolutionaries were physically annihilated.

Yet socio-economic and cultural transformations, economic successes and improvement of life standards temporarily reconciled most of the Muslims with Soviet power. Civilisational and cultural contradictions were forced underground. A double edged process developed in the national and cultural life. On the one hand the Arabic script was replaced by Roman and then Cyrillic script, religious literature was banned, most mosques and religious schools closed. Old Muslim intellectuals and *'ulama'* were executed or jailed, a certain part of the elite and intellectuals was Russified, These factors resulted in the isolation of Muslim nations from their historical and civilisational roots. On the other hand, illiteracy was eliminated, the education system developed, including higher education, a native scholarly elite emerged, as well as writers, painters, artists and other creative intellectuals with secular orientation. Furthermore bilingualism, i.e., equal command of Russian and the mother tongue, opened the door towards the world civilisation. These developments amounted to a cultural revolution, a leap over decades and sometimes centuries.

The newly formed Soviet elite of the Muslim regions became a part of the multinational all-Union *nomenklatura*. Thanks to the colossal influx of resources from Russia to the Muslim republics they began taking part in the general economic upsurge and division of labour. As for Central Russia, Tatarstan became one of the most developed regions of the country.

The disintegration of the Soviet Union began in the centre, not in the periphery. An impression arose that the post-Communist rulers, media and parties strove to spurn the Muslim regions from ethnic Russia, while the Muslims did not long for independence. Yet religious and national renaissance both in Russia and in the Muslim regions resulted in the strengthening of the elements of difference rather than of similarity and of antagonism rather than reconciliation. Russia itself is suffering an economic, social and political crisis. She has lost her national orientation and found herself ruled by the forces which are to an extent alien to her national interests.

While Russia is struggling in the search for identity, a search which is dividing intellectuals, political elite and the masses, a similar struggle is taking place among the peoples with Muslim roots in their attitude to themselves and the surrounding world. Their situation may be described as the struggle between the trends towards the Turkish and the Iranian models of development. The influence of the West of the free market and political practice attract them to the early Turkish model (preferably via Atatürk's authoritarian model). It implies that the Western path of development and progress is the only one worth copying and adapting to the local conditions. The other path is conditionally referred to as the Iranian model, to which the masses are attracted by their national values, civilisation, mythology, sentiments and state of mind. It is a declaration of return to the social structures and standards of social and individual behaviour, ideals and values elaborated in the first centuries of Islam.

Whatever may be the case, the identity of both the political elites and masses in the post-Soviet independent Muslim states is based on nationalism and Islam. It implies a certain 'repulsion' from Russia and a rise in the level of anti-Russian attitudes. But whereas nationalism draws the newly independent states to the West, Islam pulls them Eastward, or, to be accurate geographically, Southward. The post-Soviet republics have already passed after three or four years of independence through the period of euphoria caused by regaining their brothers and cousins in both the ethnic and religious sense, i.e., Turks, Iranians, Arabs, Pakistanis, etc. The period of hopes for aid from the West or 'fraternal Muslim peoples' is over. None of the hopes have materialised. Turkey, Iran, the Arab states and the West have all proved that, despite their rhetoric of support, they are pursuing their own, often egoistic ends,

Their 'aid' is limited to mosque building, Qur'an distribution, the opening of some schools, supply of TV programmes and student training. They cannot replace Russia's role economically or technically. The Soviet economy was not a single organism, but it was a single mechanism, a super-plant that consisted of organically interconnected parts. All the main transport links of the Muslim republics are orientated to Russia. The economic rupture was far more painful to them than to Russia. The local political elites were integrated into the multinational Communist administration. They used atheism as a 'religion' and promoted Russification under the slogan of 'combating nationalism'. Now the same elites are demonstrating their piousness and swearing nationalism. But nobody has forgotten their past.

The local elites have understood that neither the Turkish nor the Iranian model guarantee stability and preservation of their power and positions. The former implies a gradual transition to democracy, which the post-Soviet regimes with inherent authoritarian features cannot afford. The latter unleashes opposition forces – both counter-elites and popular masses – under the slogans of political Islam. By now, the Central Asian and Transcaucasian opposition, based on 'political Islam', has neither generally recognised charismatic leaders nor large parties. But who knows what will happen tomorrow? One thing is certain: exhortations addressed to Turkey and Iran from Central Asia and Transcaucasia ceased as early as 1992, while the need to find a common language and mutual understanding with Russia still remains.

Good relations between Russia and the Muslim republics will begin first and foremost if Russia puts her own house in order, implements socio-economic reforms and is able to begin a constructive dialogue and cooperation with her Muslim citizens and the neighbouring Muslim states. There are prerequisites for this. Russia (as well as the Soviet Union) was not an empire in the usual sense of this word. She lacked at least two main components of the characteristics of an empire: economic exploitation of the periphery by the centre and socially economically privileged position of the Russian population as compared to other peoples. With the exception of certain offices, Russians were absent in the highest echelons of the party hierarchy in the Muslim republics. They were not allowed in commerce, the most lucrative occupation. They supplied skilled and unskilled workers as well as specialists and intellectuals. But rational prerequisites do not invariably determine the socio-political behaviour of people, political elites and nations. Nationalist ideas, religious prejudices and straightforward egoism often determine relations between individuals and between nations.

There is a series of dangers involved in Russia's dialogue and cooperation with Muslim communities, peoples and states. One of these is fundamentalism which includes several interconnected elements:

exclusive appeal to the real or mythical values (religious, cultural, legal, moral, ethical, socio-political, psychological, etc.) of the community in question; contrasting 'ours' with theirs and dividing the world accordingly; stressing one's incompatibility with others; willingness to resort to violence in order to impose one's world vision and way of life on others.

Clearly this definition encompasses all kinds of fundamentalism: Muslim, Protestant, Hindu, Orthodox, liberal, Bolshevik, etc. It may be recalled that the very term fundamentalism appeared in the first decades of our century in Protestant religious literature and has no exact equivalent in Arabic or even French, (in which the term *integrisme* is used).

It is better to approach Islamic fundamentalism without hysteria. Its extremist form expresses the reaction of Islamic society and civilisation to their unequal position in the world. Colonialism has gone, but dependence on the West persists in economics, in technology, in culture, in information and in other spheres. The Soviet Union has disintegrated but dependence on Russia continues. That is why similar phenomena emerge in different countries - Muslim Brothers in Egypt, Syria and Jordan, the Islamic Salvation Front in Algeria, Jamaat-i-Islami in Pakistan and the Islamic Renaissance Party in Russia and Central Asia. The founders of Muslim fundamentalism in Russia have rarely read the works of Hasan al-Banna or Sayid Qutb, but they oppose Western values, advocate a return to 'genuine Islam', the application of Shari'a law and the creation of an Islamic state and Islamic economy with no less zeal.

But religious-political extremism has found virtually no appeal among the Russian Muslims. The Islamic Renaissance Party has become nothing more than a network of small clubs. The nationalists' slogans sound louder and are more attractive both to the elites and to the masses. In Central Asia (for instance, in Tajikistan), the party's success has been due more to clan hostility and rivalry rather than to politicisation of religion.

It is difficult to assess why fundamentalism enjoys little influence among the Russian Muslims. Possibilities include: the successful secularisation of society during the Soviet years, the rising standard of Muslim education, the emancipation of women (at least in urban areas), the prevalence of anti-fundamentalist Sufis among the Muslims of Northern Caucasia, brutal repressions against most sections of the Muslim *ulama*, the prohibition of religious literature. Finally the rupture of tradition due to the replacement of the Arabic script by the Roman and then Cyrillic script in all Muslim languages could have been a factor mitigating against fundamentalism.

Islamic fundamentalism poses no real danger to Russia. However there is a danger of extremism in the event of further aggravation of the socio-economic and inter-ethnic crisis, a danger of a higher threshold of non-perception of information, of loss of the ability to conduct a dialogue. Difficulties in mutual understanding and cooperation may also be caused by objective circumstances, too. The example of Chechnya is informative in this respect. The Russians and the Chechens are divided by the historical memory of genocide and the Chechen people suffered thrice - in the 19th century, in the 1920s and in 1940–1960s, after their mass deportation from Northern Caucasia. The people survived thanks to the clan structure of their society and spread of the Naqshbandiya and Qadiriya Sufi orders. The same structure permits a rapid seizure of socio-economic positions in the forming market economy of Russia, often by methods in conflict with the formal legal system.

However, both the Russian leaders and the self-appointed Chechen 'president' General Dudaev's inability to start a dialogue and the reluctance to compromise led to a massacre. Moscow insisted on retaining Chechnya and disarming Dudaev's, while the Chechen rebels insisted on immediate recognition of their independence. Yet the military conflict was never painted in religious colours. Dudaev's appeal for *ghazawat* (religious warfare) was not heard or supported. On the contrary, both the Muslim and the Christian clergy strove to achieve a peaceful political solution to the conflict.

Greater understanding between Muslims and non-Muslims is hampered by mutual ignorance and the spread of myths, It may be noted that entirely different notions of Muslim renaissance, pan-Islamism, Islamic fundamentalism and Sufism are lumped together in Russian socio-political thought, not to mention the media. Similarly, ignorance, combined with extreme anti-Russian or anti-Christian attitudes, creates potentially dangerous attitudes amongst Muslims. Exploiting ignorance and emotion may yield short-term dividends in politics and everyday life, but it enhances tension in confessional and ethnic relations. As a result, a constructive dialogue is replaced by a deepening conflict.

Turning to the origins, legal and behavioural standards of the Islamic civilisation creates difficulties both within a multiconfessional society and in international relations, but these difficulties do not make coexistence and cooperation impossible in principle. Many Muslim jurists 'reopen the door of *ijtihad*', i.e. they recognise the right of the *ulama* to engage in independent interpretation and judgement.

Russian society has yet to find a solution to the problems related to the revival of Islam and the reluctance of a part of citizens to obey a unified legal system which applies to every one. Social practice may ignore legal standards, for example employers taking seriously the restrictions imposed on the Muslim workforce in the month of Ramadan. The state may recognise the Muslim holidays, not to mention Muslim communities' cultural, educational and religious activities or Muslim political rights. In the long run, both the Russians and the Muslim peoples share a history not only of conflicts, but also of coexistence and mutual enrichment.

The two parties are still searching for the principles and organisational forms of coexistence. Russian Islam itself is organisationally split. There were four Muslim spiritual directorates in the USSR of which two - those of the European part of the USSR and Siberia and of Northern Caucasia - worked among the adherents of Islam in Russia. However, the old structures began disintegrating everywhere, independent spiritual directorates emerged in Tatarstan, Bashkortostan and elsewhere. Then the new directorates formed the Supreme Coordination Centre for the Russian Federation which united most of the 'young imams'. But the Moscow authorities have not yet spared even a little time to start a dialogue with this body - perhaps because Islam is not yet politicised in Russia.

The Western legal experience in relations to the colonies may also be useful in elaboration of cooperation and coexistence standards. By this I mean the application of Shari'a law amongst Muslim minorities living within the Russian state. This implies a kind of 'extraterritoriality' of some norms of Shari'a in a non-Islamic legal space.

Russia's place and role in the new world system depend on her relations not only with the West, but also with the Islamic world. She will either find an understanding and a basis for cooperation and constructive dialogue with the Muslims at home and abroad or get involved in a protracted conflict with no solution. It may cost her blood and weaken her and become a substantial factor in the disintegration of the country and undermine its capacity for self-development.

Blind imitation of the Western socio-political and economic models has already caused some dissent in Russian society. Thoughtless application of the most short-sighted views of Western politicians' may lead to a self-inflicted defeat. Russia must forge her own path of development which can cope with the modern world, as well as an approach to the Muslim world that pays due regard to her interests.

3

Dhimmi or Citizen?
Muslim-Christian Relations in Egypt

Gudrun Krämer

The treatment of minorities is generally regarded as one of the most important indications of the degree of openness, tolerance and 'modernism' of any society. The status of ethnic and religious minorities in the Muslim world has always been one of the favourite issues used to discredit Islam by the European powers who try to set themselves up as their protectors, as well as by Orientalists, including those who have appeared more critical of the interventionist approach of their rulers.

The frequently reproving attitude of Westerners, who since the 19th century have not been content with the traditional principle of toleration, but have demanded full social, political and legal equality between Muslims and non-Muslims, has provoked a defensive attitude on the part of many Muslims. In response Muslims have set about demonstrating the superiority of Islam in comparison with the Western world of Christianity, both in its values and in the way in which they are applied. As Western critics rallied against Islam as a religious, legal and social system, the defence could not be confined to exposing European pretensions, or to exposing abuses that occurred in the history of Europe as well as in current practice. It became necessary to bring into the discussion those standards and attitudes regarded as being genuinely Islamic. The policy of modernising and reform went further than this, trying to prove that Islam was in fact morally superior to the West, while at the same time being capable of adopting the universalist standards put forward by the West; in this way Islam would progress from the principle of toleration towards non-Muslims as protected subjects to that of their legal and political equality as citizens, a principle which since the age of the American and French Revolutions has been regarded as an integral part of every modern movement.[1]

The status of non-Muslims in a Muslim or Islamic society is therefore a very sensitive issue and it is not surprising that it has become strongly politicised. This is a debate in which the stakes, both real and symbolic, are very clear and which has seen the participation, in the past and in the present, of 'ulama', both traditional and reformist, 'enlightened' intellectuals and militant absolutists, defenders of the government and their opponents, indigenous and immigrant non-Muslims, foreign observers and Orientalists. This debate illustrates, possibly better than others, the logic and modalities of the Islamic reform movement, as well as its limits and limitations.

Classical Legal Doctrines

Pre-modern Islamic ideas on the status of non-Muslims in Islamic lands are too well known to be dealt with in detail here.[2] In part they are based on Qur'anic texts, which are often ambiguous and contradictory. These reflect quite faithfully the development of relations between the Muslim community, at first vulnerable and threatened, then increasingly confident and aware of itself with its non-Muslim neighbours, both Christians and Jews. These relations changed from co-operation, under the direction of a prophet hoping to be recognised by upholders of the monotheistic tradition, into hostility and armed struggle when he saw that he was denied this recognition and support. From the earliest days, therefore, we see the results of this conflict between practice and theory, which characterises relations between believers and non-believers.[3]

The principal themes of the Qur'anic texts are the supremacy of the Muslim community both in this world and the next and the possibility of good relations or even of friendship (muwalat) between Muslims and non-Muslims. In this respect, these texts establish a principle based on reaction: it is the behaviour of non-Muslims towards Muslims which determines their status and treatment. So long as they behave themselves, they will be treated with justice, mercy and fairness. Otherwise, they will be attacked until they recognise the dominance of Islam and the Muslims. If it is easy to explain this principle by reference to the relations between the various powers existing in the time of the Prophet and the 'rightly guided' Caliphs (*rashidun*), it is very significant that it should be revived in the language of contemporary Islamic militants, such as the members of the al-Jihad group, who in a situation which has changed radically in favour of Muslims, seek to make this principle the rule governing all co-habitation between Muslims and Christians in Egypt We will return to this subject later.

The principle of reaction is not so obvious in the classical legal doctrines, where behind the rigid dichotomies which divide the world into clearly delimited and even antagonistic parts, (*dar al-Islam* and *dar al-harb* as far as land is concerned, and believers and non-believers for the inhabitants), we see those subtle distinctions which are so characteristic of Islamic law (*fiqh*), between different categories of believers and non-believers. As its authority spread beyond the Christian, Jewish, Sabean and Zoroastrian (*majus*) communities of its first period, Islam ceased to recognise the distinction between polytheistic pagans (*kuffar*, sing. *kafir*) and the people of the monotheistic book (*ahl al-Kitab*), whose faith is based on revelation. For some schools of Islamic law, the status of pagans (animists in Arabia, or at the present time in the Sudan; Buddhists and Hindus in India, etc.) was in practice merged with those of the people of the book. They all enjoyed a situation of toleration and protection, in principle unlimited, and guaranteed by a contract (*dhimmah*). As a sign of their submission to the Islamic authority they were obliged to pay tribute and special taxes, in particular the *jizyah* and the *kharaj*.

In short, this amounted to a condition of toleration and contractual protection which did not question the supremacy of the Muslim community which would find its true reward in the world to come but which should, however, be expressed already in this world by social and political domination. Looked at in more detail, the differences between the various law schools regarding the rights and obligations of the protected non-Muslims (*dhimmis*) were considerable. Among these, the Hanafi School, dominant in the Ottoman Empire, but not among the population of Egypt which for the most part followed the Shafi'i school, was the most liberal, making provision even in the areas of property and penal law (with the exception of the 'canonical' punishments, *hudud*) for complete equality between Muslims and non-Muslims.

At the same time, it seems fair to point out that the doctors of Islamic law tended to draw quite distinct boundaries between Muslims and non-Muslims, and to interpret the subjection of *dhimmis* to Islamic authority as a justification for discriminatory and humiliating measures imposed upon them. This principle was based upon a well-known verse in the Qur'an[4] and upon the agreement, known as the covenant of Umar and attributed to the second 'rightly guided' Caliph, Umar ibn al-Khattab (634–644), but probably drawn up some time in the 8th century.[5] Practice, however, did not always conform to the rigorous prescriptions of the jurists and to popular ideas of superiority. In practice, the treatment of non-Muslims was closely dependent on economic, social and political conditions in the territory of any particular ruler, on their usefulness to him, and on his relations with the principal neighbouring non-Muslim powers – Byzantines, Mongols, or Crusaders in the classical era, European powers, Zionists and the state of Israel in modern times. Having said this, legal ideas, even if not applied, always remained the point of reference for the attitudes and expectations of Muslims. If, at any given moment, non-Muslims, or, what was more usual, certain members of their élite, enjoyed conditions more favourable than those set down by the *'ulama*, this was regarded as an essentially illegal deviation, and not as a modification of the theory in the light of reality, as the result of changing relations between the powers, or standards and values. Once the historical circumstances which led to their formulation no longer applied, and they became ossified and rooted in the collective memory, the rules of the *fiqh* took on the force of the *shari'ah*. Accordingly, modern reformers seek to free them from their historicity which is now dead and buried.

Reform, Emancipation, Complications

Traditional ideas were still in full force, when from the middle of the 19th century onwards the provisions of Islamic law were increasingly replaced by new laws adopted from man-made law which was intended to free the protected non-Muslims, the *dhimmis*, and to make them full citizens, *muwatinun*. The abolition in Egypt of discriminatory measures imposed in the name of the 'Covenant of 'Umar', as well as, for a very limited period during the French Expedition (1798–1801) of the *jizya* have left few traces. At this time, exporting the principle of equality was not yet part of France's Egyptian policy.[6] The recruitment into the army by Muhammad Ali of a certain number of Copts after 1820 was dictated by the need to find soldiers, and not by any desire to build up a national community on the basis of equality.[7] It was only the administrative and legal reforms of the Ottoman Empire, the Tanzimat, culminating in the edicts of 1839 and 1856, which under strong European pressure, established equality before the law for all the Sultan's subjects. In Egypt, the *jizya* was abolished by the Khedive Sa'id in 1855, followed in 1856 by a more widespread recruitment of Copts for military service. Fifty years later, the 'Revolution of 1919' seemed to signal the victory of equality and national unity over religious separatism ('Religion for God, and the Fatherland for all').

The principle of equality was enshrined in the Egyptian constitution of 1923, which, while declaring Islam to be the official religion of the state, did not establish the *shari'ah* as the principal or exclusive source of legislation. It did not, however, provide for the proportional representation of non-Muslim minorities.[8] It was thus the opposite of the Lebanese system, which based the political and administrative organisation of society on the basis of proportional representation, in this way reinforcing confessional ties and feelings of solidarity within different communities (ta'ifiyya).[9] In the 1950s this was to explode into civil war.

Legal emancipation, however, did not mean the same thing as cultural assimilation or the political integration of non-Islamic communities[10] into the Egyptian nation which was being created, and was seeking to define its identity.[11] Nor was it accompanied by the drawing up of a unified national legal system. On the contrary, it was in the 19th century that the cultural and legal autonomy of non-Muslim communities reached its apogee within the administrative framework of the *millets*. By classifying citizens according to their religion and nominating members of the ecclesiastical hierarchies as their official representatives, this system strengthened the feeling of solidarity within, and divisions between, different communities. This was expressed above all by upholding religious legislation in matters of family law (the status of individuals).[12] Thus it was that the multiplication of legal codes and tribunals reached its peak in the 19th century.

Turning to the cultural assimilation and the social and political integration of non-Muslims into Egyptian society under the more or less direct control of Great Britain, it is not only necessary to recognise distinctions between the Copts[13] and the other minorities, whether settled in the country for centuries or immigrants of more recent date. Among the latter, in particular, class distinctions and levels of education largely determined their economic, social and political status. There were cosmopolitan people prominent in society and a polyglot middle class, mainly attached to the colonial economic sector, and in any case closely identified with it. In social and political matters they often felt closer to their own particular community or to Europe than to their Muslim compatriots. But side by side with them, and often neglected, were the poorer classes, who for the most part spoke Arabic, and had mainly adopted Egyptian ways and customs. As they were dependent upon their richer and better educated co-religionists for education, help and charity, they often led a more withdrawn life than the latter, and in general they took as little part in the intellectual and political life of the country as their Muslim or Coptic compatriots.[14]

Compared to the medieval and pre-colonial eras, at the beginning of the 19th century one is aware of a large variety of roles and economic and social functions within the different communities, as well as a certain diversification of cultural, intellectual and political interests, both among individuals and whole communities. As for their position within Egyptian society, they enjoyed emancipation; certain groups and individuals had legal and economic privileges granted or upheld by the European powers. This period saw the end of the *millet* system as the framework for political and administrative relations between Muslims and non-Muslims, but not the end of religion as an important source of solidarity, and occasionally of collective action. The slow dissolution of this religious and 'ethnic division of work', which had characterised the pre-colonial society and economy could be seen. At the same time, however, one sees the effects of a two-fold process of marginalising the non-Muslims. While in the course of a long period of development, the Copts had been reduced to a minority, all the other minorities had, rightly or wrongly, been regarded as foreigners. Although right up to the time of Egypt's (formal) independence in 1922, Copts continued to fulfil important functions in administration and economics as well as in culture and language, they had either been discredited because of their association with the occupying power, or else disputed by a new Egyptian Islamic middle class.

Islamic Reformist Debates

Although the status of non-Muslims within Islam in general, and within the ideal Islamic order (*al-nizam al-islami*) in particular, is a subject of discussion within the Islamic reformist debate of the 20th century, the actual state of affairs in Egypt is not discussed. This makes the debate somewhat unreal and often unhistorical. For those Muslims who are looking for an 'Islamic' solution to the problems of their society, it was, and still is, a question of either appropriating the achievements of the past (i.e. the emancipation of non-Muslims and their recognition as full citizens) and of justifying them in Islamic terms, or else of reversing them in the name of a particularist form of Islamic legitimacy (i.e. the reaffirmation of *dhimma* as the basis of co-existence between the various religious communities).

In theory, at least, this latter programme is the simpler. This was the recommendation of the Muslim Brotherhood during the 1930s and 1940s, and is the demand, with even greater violence, of contemporary militant radicals who seek to re-impose segregation between believers and non-believers, and to marginalise the latter both economically and politically. Modern reformers take a different view. For them it is a question of affirming and re-establishing in daily life those religious values which have long since ceased to be upheld, and to show that, provided they are 'correctly' interpreted and applied, they would be compatible with the principle of equality. Faced with the challenge of traditional standards, which are particularist and restrictive, and the modern, universalist demands which oppose them, the path of the Islamic modernist is an extremely difficult one.

This question lies at the heart of the debate on the nationalist programme and the programme of religious reform. Both these forces seek to bring about the unity and authentic identity of the community and to defend it against cultural and political aggression emanating from external sources. But although they have certain important goals in common, they remain deeply divided as to the basis for belonging to this community, the Egyptian nation or Islamic *ummah*. In fact, the dilemma can be solved so far as the great majority of Sunni Muslims are concerned. However, it remains very much an issue for the Christian Copts, who are natives of the country, indisputably Egyptians. This problem continued to exist in the inter-war period, even more acutely for those minorities of non-Egyptian origin, and in particular for non-Muslims.

Although legal emancipation has been in force for over a century, the principle of legal and political equality for non-Muslims continues to create problems for the *'ulama* and Islamic militants. It should be noted that in their theoretical pronouncements they make no distinction between the Copts (and Jews), who are genuinely Egyptian and Syrian, Armenian, Greek, Italian and Jewish immigrants. It is not that they question the value and dignity of each man (and woman) as descendants of Adam, that is to say as human beings (on the basis of the relevant Qur'anic verses, in particular 4:1 and 17:70, reflected in the concept of man as the viceroy of God on earth, *istikhlaf*).[15] This idea, which is recognised almost universally, could serve as a genuinely Islamic basis for the concept of human rights.[16] However, it does not necessarily mean the legal and political equality of all men (and women), and this is where the problem arises. It is to be noted that in reformist considerations legal details (the right to bear witness, the calculation of *diyah*, etc.) and the discriminatory regulations of the classical textbooks (the prohibitions on bearing arms, on wearing sumptuous apparel, on horse riding, on building new churches and synagogues, etc.) are no longer of interest to them. They are preoccupied with the political sphere.

The slogan which is most often cited is 'equal rights and equal obligations' (*lahum ma lana wa-'alaihim ma 'alaina*). This slogan is based on the Hanafi tradition and at first sight appears to correspond with the principle of equality. However, our authors are at pains to add that it has to do with an equality which respects the religious autonomy of non-Muslims, and which allows them to keep their special identity, defined with respect to religion. The defense of religious legislation affecting the status of the individual is presented as a measure offering protection against alienation.[18] In this way there will be equality in all spheres, except that of religion – a situation that is at the same time very important, and very problematic. Once more one is faced here with the distinction between what has to do with religion in the narrow sense (essentially, the area of worship, *'ibadah*[19]), and with relations between people (*mu'amalat*, i.e. family, economic and political life). Apart from the restrictive framework of divine authoritative injunctions (*nass qati' al-dalala*), which are considered to be immutable and inviolable, these are regarded as being subject to change, according to the exigencies of place and time. Thus they remain to be defined according to the on-going interaction between Islamic principles and changing circumstances (exigencies, constraints, possibilities). In this distinction drawn between what contemporaries call 'the fixed' elements (*al-thabit*), containing the hard core of Islam, and its 'flexible' elements (*al-mutaghayyir*), can be seen the mark of the Western distinction between the sacred and the profane, the spiritual and temporal. This can be seen in one form or another in all reformers from Muhammad Abduh to Yusuf al-Qaradawi,[20] even if they continue to maintain with all their force that, unlike Christianity, Islam is both religion and state, religion and the world (*al-islam din wa-daula*).[21] They see no contradiction in this, because there is no total separation between religion and politics (a secularist idea which is condemned by all Islamic reformers) nor the complete fusion which they envisage, but rather a harmonious balance between two different spheres, both of which, however, remain subject to divine law.[22]

As far as the position of non-Muslims in Islamic society is concerned, everything clearly depends on what is considered to be relevant to the sphere of religion. In the present case, the contentious issue is primarily the classification of the major functions of the Islamic state, a state founded on a religious or even ideological basis (*daulat fikra, daulat risala, daula 'aqa'idiyya*), and having as its principal purpose the fulfilment of the general interest (*al-maslaha al-'amma*) of the Islamic community in this world and the salvation of every Muslim in the world to come. Seen from this perspective, it seems logical to Islamic reformers that non-believers, who are not obliged to observe every detail of the *shari'ah*, which serves as the ideological basis of the state, should be excluded from all responsibility connected with its application. At the same time it should confer upon Muslims power (*wilaya*), such as the functions of caliph or judge, and the fulfilment of religious duties such as *jihad*, the collection and distribution of alms (*zakat*) and the overseeing of Islamic standards and values (*hisba*).[23]

If, in opposition to radicals such as the Indo-Pakistani Abu'l-A'la al-Maududi (1903–79), the Egyptian Sayyid Qutb (1906–66) and their disciples, the reformers admit non-Muslims to nationality in the Islamic state (*al-jinsiyya al-islamiyya*), as well as granting them the right to vote, they persist in denying them important political, legal and military functions. Thus there would be universal suffrage, but only Muslims could be elected to office. If nearly all of them make use of the term '*muwatin*', it is in the literal sense of 'compatriot', and not of 'citizen', enjoying the full civil and political rights associated with Islamic nationality.[24] Following this logic, non-Muslims living in the same territory, can quite well be '*muwatinun*', and at the same time '*dhimmiyyun*', in other words, protected compatriots, but not necessarily citizens in the full sense of the word. It is the idea of justice ('*adl*, '*adala*, *qist*) which gives each individual what is his right (without this necessarily being the same for all), and which takes precedence over the idea of equality (*musawat*). One comes up against this in the same way when discussing the status of women 'in Islam'.

The ideas of Hasan al-Banna (1906–49), founder and 'supreme guide' of the Association of Muslim Brothers, is a good example of the more or less traditional and moralising approach. Al-Banna deals with the question of non-Islamic minorities as one of ethics and values (an appeal to the spirit of justice, to the piety and mercy of Muslims, to the brotherhood of all believers, and to understanding between the different elements of the Egyptian nation), rather than as a political and legal question, (which would require a systematic consideration of *dhimma* and equality).[25] The distinction drawn between the Coptic minority, on the one hand, recognised as being genuinely Egyptian, and the other minorities of Arab or European origin, who hardly figure at all in the more or less theoretical pronouncements, became evident however in practice. It was, of course, a political distinction, based on the hope of forging a common front against the British occupation force, in the case of the Copts, and on contempt and antagonism, in the case of the Jews, who ever since the end of the 1930s had been regarded as the fifth column of the Zionist enemy.[26] The pressure exerted by the Muslim Brotherhood in favour of the wholesale application of the Shar'iah, reminded the Copts of their former humiliation. It revived their fear of the re-introduction of the *jizyah*, and so strictly limited the possibilities of mutual understanding.

However, there are many voices attempting to go beyond the more or less traditional view of relations between Muslims and non-Muslims within a national community which has an Islamic majority, and which consequently takes its inspiration from Islamic standards and values.[27] Their approach to the problem of equality is similar to that of other religious reformers. This consists of an historical and functional analysis of Islamic law (*fiqh*), the tradition of the Prophet, the Sunnah, and of the Qur'an, in an attempt to reduce to a minimum the positive regulations of the Shar'iah (*nass*), and return instead to what they call its highest principles and values (*maqasid al-shari'ah*). Verses from the Qur'an are placed in the context of their revelation (*asbab annuzul*) with the intention of minimising as far as possible their validity for the circumstances of present-day reality. Thus friendship and good relations, not hostility and contempt between Muslims and non-Muslims, (provided the latter are not openly hostile to believers), are endorsed as the principle rule of co-existence. This is contrary to the views of Qutb and Maududi, who seek to make exclusivity and religious discrimination the basic principle of all social and political organisation within the Islamic state.[28]

Following this logic, the *jizyah* – a symbol of religious discrimination and humiliation, deeply rooted in the memory of non-Muslims – becomes a once-for-all tax granting exemption from military service, a principle which is confirmed by the practice of the Companions of the Prophet and the 'rightly guided' Caliphs. In other words, the *salaf salih*, held in high respect by every Islamic reformer and militant Muslim, as well as by the practice of Muhammad Ali, in a more recent period. More daringly, the *jihad* becomes the struggle for national liberation in which Muslims and non-Muslims have taken part. Memories of the 1919 Revolution, as well as of the co-operation of Muslims, Copts and other minorities in the Wafd Party, serve to reinforce this idea.[29] The historical distinction between different ways of incorporating non-Muslims into the Islamic state (*sulhan* or *'anwatan*, i.e. through agreement or by military force) has quite simply been declared obsolete and irrelevant to the contemporary situation. On the other hand, the sacred principle of those who held power and the learned doctors in the classical era, i.e. that of avoiding all disorder and all strife (*fitnah*) in order to maintain the unity of the community, is raised to the highest rank. Since 1919, and again since the 1970s, it has been *fitnah ta'ifiyyah*, confessional violence tearing apart the national fabric, which must be avoided and combated at all cost. However, it is no longer the Islamic community which is to be defended, but the national, inter-confessional union. In the same way, the general interest (*al-maslaha al-'amma*) invoked in every situation of tension and crisis is defined by reference to the community – political, national and Egyptian.

More recently, and going still further, several modernist intellectuals and jurists, (such as Tariq al-Bishri), who are close to the moderate and even enlightened Islamic movement, have adopted a functional analysis. Dealing with public functions, this takes the institutions and structures of the modern state as its starting point, rather than the person of the functionary.[30] According to them it is no longer individuals who make laws and take decisions, but groups and organisations, which are all subject to a supreme law and a unified legal system. Impeccable logic – which is based, however, on a fundamental condition: that the law in itself does not contain any clauses that discriminate against any elements in the nation, whether they be non-Muslims, women, or all the members of certain social strata or classes. At the same time, it is a logic far removed from the reformist ideas of the 1920s, 1930s and 1940s, making a complete break with the personalist, casuistic approach of classical Islamic law.

Conclusion

Efforts to establish, on a genuinely Islamic foundation, the principle of legal and political equality between Muslims and non-Muslims as inhabitants, and even more, as citizens of the same country, have increased since the end of the 19th century. The dilemma remains, however, of a reformist plan which tries to ensure identity and authenticity, both individual and collective, while appealing to the religious and legal core of Islam, which represents not only a definitive revelation, but at the same time provides the majority of the nation with its religion. A religious and legal core, however, which, before being able to fulfil this goal, must be radically re-interpreted in the light of modern circumstances and universalist, egalitarian aspirations. In the case under discussion, only a rigorous distinction between the Shari'ah and Islamic law can contribute to this; for it is only a Shari'ah systematically stripped, as a result of historical and functional analysis, of all discriminatory references contained in the classic law which was developed with the express aim of assuring the spiritual and political supremacy of the Muslim community, which could serve to bring about the two-fold aim of cultural authenticity and national unity. The colonial period clearly demonstrated the need for this. It still remains to be achieved, however – and to be firmly integrated into reformist Islamic thought and practice.

Notes

1.   It should be noted in passing that in flagrant violation of this principle, neither granted equal legal and political status to women or slaves.

2.   For thorough examinations of this subject, see Antoine Fattal, *Le Statut légal des non-musulmans en pays d'Islam*, Beirut, 1958; 'Abd al-Karim Zaydan, *Ahkam al-dhimmiyyin wal-musta'minin fi dar al-islam*, s.l., 1963; or Adel Khoury, *Toleranz im Islam*, Munich & Mainz, 1980. For a more historical analysis, see Albrecht Noth, 'Möglichkeiten und Grenzen islamischer Toleranz', in: *Saeculum*, (Freiburg), 29, (1978), pp.190–204.

3.   The same dialectical logic is seen in the studies of Middle Eastern Christian minorities outside Egypt. See in particular Robert B. Betts, *Christians in the Arab East*, Atlanta and London, 1975; and John Joseph, *Muslim-Christian relations and inter-Christian rivalries in the Middle East: the case of the Jacobites in an age of transition*, Albany, 1983; see also Youssef Courbage & Philippe Fargues, *Christians and Jews under Islam*, London, 1997.

4.   This refers to Surah 9:29, ('Tauba' = Repentance): 'Fight against such of those to whom the Scriptures were given as believe neither in God nor the Last Day ... until they pay tribute [*jizyah*] out of hand and are utterly subdued (*wa -hum saghirun*).

5.   For the latter, see the study, detailed but unhistorical and badly organised, by A. S. Tritton: *The Caliphs and their non-Muslim Subjects*, London, 1930. For an historian's approach, see Albrecht Noth, 'Abgrenzungsprobleme zwischen Muslimen und Nicht-Muslimen: die 'Bedingungen 'Umars (*assurut al- 'umariyya*)' unter anderem Aspekt gelesen', *Jerusalem Studies in Arabism and Islam*, 9, (1987), pp. 290–315.

6.   Harald Motzki, *Dimma und Égalité: die nichtmuslimischen Minderheiten Ägyptens in der zweiten Hälfte des 18. Jahr- hunderts und die Expedition Bonapartes (1798–1801)*, Bonn, 1979, pp. 160f, 170–72, 266f, 317ff.

7.   See Tariq al-Bishri, *Al-muslimum wal-aqbat fi itar al-jama'a al-wataniyya*, Cairo, 1980, pp.83ff; and, Afaf Lutfi al-Sayyid Marsot, *Egypt in the Reign of Muhammad Ali*, Cambridge, 1984, pp.128–32 (130).

8.   For the growth of Egyptian nationality, closely linked with the question of minorities, see Frédéric Abecassis & Ann Le Gall-Kazazian, 'L'identité au miroir du droit – le statut des personnes en Egypte (fin XIXe – milieu XXe siècle)', in *Egypte/Monde arabe*, 11, (3/1992), pp.11–38.

9.   For an analysis of the strength of community and family particularism, and of national cohesion, see the thorough study by Theodor Hanf, *Coexistence in Wartime Lebanon: Decline of a State and Rise of a Nation*, London, 1993.

10.   We will not attempt to trace here the development of the different non-Muslim communities established in Egypt in the 19th and 20th centuries, which have been the subject of a considerable and growing number of studies, dealing not only with the Coptic community with its different

religious components (Orthodox, Catholic and Protestant), but also the Syrian, Greek, Italian, Armenian, Jewish (both rabbinical and Karaite). Still lacking, however, is a comparative study, which analyses the common features (reform in society and internal politics, linked to the growth in the first quarter of the 19th century of a middle class, comfortably off and cultivated, which fought against the dominant position of the clergy and other prominent people within their community; educational and language reform, the struggle against religious legislation affecting personal status, which was defended by the clergy as the last bastion against an irresistible secularisation, but also the (re-)mobilisation of communal strategies in times of crisis, etc.), a synthesis which will not overlook the deep divisions in the status, orientation and interests of these communities (especially between the Copts, and – this is often ignored – the Jews on the one hand, and minorities, both Muslim and non-Muslim, but of non-Egyptian origin, on the other.)

11.   Among the large number of detailed and thorough studies, see Israel Gershoni & James P. Jankowski, *Egypt, Islam and the Arabs: the search for Egyptian nationhood, 1900–1930*, New York, 1986; and for a wider approach, Alain Roussillon, 'Egyptianité, arabité, islamité: la recomposition des référents identitaires', in: *Egypte/Monde arabe*, 11, (3/1992), pp.77–132.

12.   For the development of the *millets*, see Benjamin Braude & Bernard Lewis,(eds) *Christians and Jews in the Ottoman Empire: the functioning of a plural society*, 2 vol, New York, 1982. For the status of individuals, see, Muhammad Mahmud Nammar & Alfi Butrus Habashi, *Al-ahwal al-shakhsiyya li'l-tawa'if ghair al-islamiyya min al-misriyyin (fi al-shari'atain al-masihiyya wa'l-musawiyya)*, Cairo, 1957.

13.   For the history and growth of the Copt community, see especially al-Bishri, *Al-muslimun wa'l-aqbat*, (which is still regarded as a reference work by all Egyptian authors); Barbara L.Carter, *The Copts in Egyptian politics, 1919–1952*, London, 1985; Rafiq Habib, *Al-ihya' al-dini: milaff ijtima'i li'l-tayyarat al-masihiyya wa'l-islamiyya fi misr*, Cairo, 1991; and the article by Dina El Khawaga, 'Le développement communautaire copte: un mode de partici- pation au politique?', in: *Monde arabe, Maghreb–Machrek*, 135, (1991), pp.3–18.

14.   I refer to my own study of the Jews in Egypt, *The Jews in Modern Egypt, 1914–1952*, Seattle & London, 1989. However, the Jews cannot be taken as representative of the non- Muslim communities established in Egypt, and whose degree of cultural assimilation and political integration was markedly different from that of the indigenous Copts. For the education, interests and policies of the upper bourgeoisie, Muslim as well as non-Muslim, see Robert Tignor, 'The economic activities of foreigners in Egypt, 1920–1950: from Millet to Haute Bourgeoisie', in *Comparative Studies in Society and History*, 22, (1980), pp. 416–49.

15.   An interesting formulation, and one which is often reprinted, of this idea which represents man as the regent of God on earth, is found in the

work of the jurist and prominent member of the Muslim Brotherhood 'Abd al-Qadir 'Auda, *Al-islam wa-auda'una al-siyasiyya*, Cairo, n.d. (written about 1950 or 1951), especially pp. 9ff, 19–23, 184, 279ff.

16. We will not deal here with the very delicate and contro versial issue of human rights 'in Islam'. See, for example, Ali Merad, 'Le concept de 'droits de l'homme' en Islam: réflexions sur la déclaration islamique universelle des droits de l'homme', Université de Tunis, CERES, *IIIème Rencontre Islamo-Chrétienne: Droits de l'homme*, Tunis, 1985, pp. 243–60.

17. This is in contrast to contemporary militant Islamists who continue to show a great interest in this topic. It should be noted that many of the cases of religious violence (*fitna ta'ifiyya*) have been linked with disputes over the building of churches and mosques.

18 One cannot see in this the defence of the interests of a particular religious group, which was so evident in the case of the Christian and Jewish clergy, whose tenacious hold on religious juridiction in the sphere of individual status can be explained more easily in view of the growth since the end of the 19th century of a new lay élite with a secular orientation, and which fought with the clergy for control of community affairs. See, for example, Abecassis & Le Gal-Kazazian, op.cit., pp. 27ff. For the Copts, see al-Bishri, op. cit., especially pp. 391–467; and for the Jews, Krämer, G., op. cit., pp. 68–115.

19. Also known as the Five Pillars of Islam: the profession of faith (*shahadah*), prayer, fasting during the month of Ramadan, the giving of alms (*zakah*), and pilgrimage to Mecca. Some people add to these a Sixth Pillar, the duty to fight along the path of God (*al-jihad fi sabil Allah*).

20. Yusuf al-Qaradawi, an Egyptian member of the Muslim Brotherhood, Professor of Islamic Law at the University of Qatar at Doha, and since the 1960s one of the stars of the Islamist movement in the Arab world; see, for example, the discussions with the author, published by Yasir Farahat, *Humum al-muslim al-mu'asir fi fikr al-da'iya al-islamiyya al-duktur Yusuf al-Qaradawi*, Cairo, 1988.

21. The only people to reject this are those who advocate the exclusive sovereignty of God (*hakimiyyat allah*), Maududi and Qutb and their contemporary followers.

22. There is quite a clear presentation of this in the works of Muhammad 'Ammara (often referred to as 'Imara), who regards himself as the disciple, and perhaps the intellectual heir, of 'Abduh, whose complete works he has published; see especially his study, *Al-daula al-islamiyya baina al-'almaniyya wa'l-sulta al-diniyya*, Cairo & Beirut, 1988.

23. For the positions of the various groups and thinkers, see the articles by Nabil 'Abd al-Fattah, 'Al-islam wa'l- aqalliyyat al-diniyya fi misr: al-tayyarat wa'l- ishkaliyyat', in *al-Mustaqbal al-'Arabi*, 30, (8/1981), pp. 92–113; Nivin 'Abd al-Mun'im Mus'ad, 'Al-tayyarat al- diniyya fi misr wa-qadiyyat al-aqalliyyat', *ibid.*, 119 (1/1989), pp. 90–119, and Fahmi Huwaidi, 'Al-sahwa

al- islamiyya wa'l-muwatana wa'l-musawat', in *al-Hiwar*, 7 (autumn 1987), pp.53–70.

24.   The use of this term is justified by Yusuf al-Qaradawi in his treatise, *Ghair al-muslimin fi al-mujtama' al-islami*, 4th ed., Beirut, 1985, pp.5ff.

25.   See especially his circulars, 'A la jeunesse' (*ila al-shabab*), and 'Notre mission' (*da'watuna*), *Majmu'at rasa'il al-imam al-shahid Hasan al-Banna*, n.p.,n.d., pp. 19–23, 69f, 78–89. Note in passing that the problem is virtually ignored in the detailed, but uncritical, study by Ibrahim al-Bayyumi Ghanim, *Al-fikr al-siyasi li'l-imam Hasan al-Banna*, Cairo, 1992, even though he describes at length the role of the Muslim Brotherhood in the Egyptian national movement (pp. 301–4 and 403ff). A master's thesis presented to the University of Tanta in 1989, and subsequently published by an Islamic publishing house can serve as an introduction to the teachings and practices of the Muslim Brotherhood: 'Uthman 'Abd al-Mut'izz Raslan, *At-tarbiya al-siyasiyya 'inda jama'at al-ikhwan al-muslimin fi al-fatra min 1928 ila 1954 m fi misr. Dirasa tahliliyya taqwimiyya*, Cairo, n.d., especially pp. 273ff.

26.   For relations with the Copts, see Zakariya Sulaiman al- Bayyumi, *Al-ikhwan al-muslimun wa'l-jama'at al-islamiyya fi al-hayat al-siyasiyya al-misriyya, 1928–1948*, Cairo, 1979, pp. 311–18; and al-Bishri, *Al-muslimun wa'l-aqbat*, pp.496–516; for the Jews, see Krämer, op. cit., pp. 139ff.

27.   What follows is based on the most recent writings, such as the detailed study of the Azharist Zaydan, *Ahkam al-dhimmiyyin*, and the more deliberately reformist approaches such as those of Yusuf al-Qaradawi, *Ghair al-muslimin fi al-mujtama' al-islami*; of the very 'enlightened' jurist Muhammad Salim al-'Awwa, 'An-nizam al-islami wa-wad' ghair al-muslimin', in *al-Hiwar*, 5, (1987), pp. 41–57, and, *idem.*, *Al-aqbat wa'l-islam*, Cairo, 1987; or of the journalist, close to the moderate Islamist movement, Fahmi Huwaidi, *Muwatinun ... la dhimmiyyun. Mauqi' ghair al-muslimin fi mujtama' al-muslimin*, Beirut & Cairo, 1985. The origins and development of the historical, functional approaches still need to be established with much more precision in the way that they are applied to the question of non-Muslims in Egypt and/or in Islamic society.

28.   See, for example, Huwaidi, 'Al-sahwa al-islamiyya', pp. 61–3; Mus'ad, 'Al-tayyarat al-diniyya', *passim*, and Habib, *Al-ihya' al-dini*, pp. 212–7. Attention has often been drawn to the political reasons for this antagonism, which, while attacking the Copts, seeks to undermine the credibility, both inside and outside the country, of the Egyptian government which is failing to protect the national union; for the complexities of this game, see Hamied N. Ansari, 'Sectarian conflict and the political expediency of religion', *Middle East Journal*, 38, (1983), 3, pp.123–44. It is Rafiq Habib who, during the 1970s and 1980s tried to analyse more systematically the economic and social causes of inter-religious tension (*fitna ta'ifiyya*): *Al-ihtijaj al- dini wa'l-sira' al-tabaqi fi misr*, Cairo, 1989.

29.   See, besides the studies by al-Bishri or Carter, the works of Abu Saif

Yusuf, especially his study, *Al-aqbat wa'l- qaumiyya al-'arabiyya (dirasa istitla'iyya)*, Beirut, 1987.

30. See, for example, his communication at the conference of nationalists and Islamists organised in Cairo in September 1989: Markaz dirasat al-wahda al-'arabiyya, (ed.), *Al-hiwar al-qaumi al-dini*, Beirut, 1989, pp. 139f.

4

Central Asia:
from Communism to Democracy and Islam?

Aleksei Malashenko

When one discusses the prospects for democracy in the Muslim regions of the former USSR, including the Central Asian states, it is necessary first of all to have an idea of the type of society that formed during the years of Soviet power and still exists today. There are two points of view on this matter. The main elements of the totalitarian system have been preserved in Central Asia to a greater extent than in Russia and other Slav republics, not to mention Transcaucasia and the Baltic region. The Soviet mentality has proved more stable there than anywhere else and Communist mythologies still prevail in the social consciousness . According to this logic, the main obstacles to the creation of a democratic society are the surviving, though modified, Communist structures and institutions. Many Russian politicians and journalists support this view, especially those who participate in the struggle for human rights and support the local democratic groups. Until the middle of 1993 the view also prevailed in the Russian Ministry of Foreign Affairs.

The essence of the second view, represented by many Russian scholars, including experts in religion and Orientalists, among them L. S. Vasiliev, B. S. Erasov, L. R. Polonskaya, S. P. Polyakov and others, is that the traditional society, though in a modified form, remains intact in the Muslim regions of the former USSR, with the exception of Tatarstan (Tataria) and Bashkortostan (Bashkiria). In spite of the considerable changes that occurred in the years of Soviet power, Islam continues to strongly influence society.

The attitude of Islam and the Muslim political culture to the

European variant of democracy has generally been negative. Islamic political thought combined with the Muslim peoples' national traditions, are not conducive to the spread of democratic (in a European understanding) traditions and standards of social and political behaviour in society. It is indisputable that Communism played an immensely negative role in suppressing democratic processes in traditional Muslim society in the Soviet Union. However, it is no less true that the failure of democratic processes in Central Asia is possibly primarily caused by deep rooted features of that society, of which the following seem most important:

1. The priority of the collective over the interests and freedom of the individual, resulting in his or her submission to the collective - whether it be kin, clan or the Muslim community as a whole
2. The authoritarian character of state power, which ensures the community's interests and stability;
3. The low level of secularisation, particularly the incomplete separation of secular and spiritual powers; theocratic or quasi-theocratic trends are peculiar to many or even most Muslim countries: the secular head of the state often becomes the nation's 'spiritual father', which was exemplified by Habib Bourguiba and Gamal Abdel Nasser, the late Egyptian leader, and today by Islam Karimov, president of Uzbekistan, and Saparmurat Niyazov, the president of Turkmenistan.

In a certain sense, similar trends to those mentioned above are also found in Russian society with inherent collectivist attitudes, authoritarian power and influence of religion on politics. Consequently it could be argued that Soviet power proved in a sense organic to Muslim society, which managed to adapt itself to it. The main institutions of the traditional society continued functioning under that power, and social relations changed little.[1].

It should be noted that, unlike the Muslims of the Middle East and South Asia, the peoples of Central Asia had little or no acquaintance with Western democratic institutions when they became subjects of the Russian empire. They were further deprived of that opportunity under the Communist system with its 'iron curtain' and full immunity from any manifestations of democracy.

Simultaneously the Muslims of the Soviet Union were isolated from the nucleus of the Muslim world, where processes of modernisation of society and partial reformation of Islam began at the end of the past century, making it more open to contacts with the European civilisation. The process of religious reformation was artificially interrupted in Central Asia, as well as in other regions of 'Soviet Islam'. The local spiritual elite was to a great extent exterminated by the early 1940s.

It was noted above that underdevelopment of democracy (in the European understanding) in the post-Soviet Muslim regions is a generally natural phenomenon in a Muslim traditional society. At the same time, while restraining its members' individualist tendencies and keeping them dependent on the community, traditional society left a 'reserve' for individuals' self-expression. There was a stratum, though a relatively tiny one, of intellectuals in traditional society which allowed a degree of independent thought. Conflict arose between the state and personality, between the community and its individual members. One may say that there are specific forms of democracy in Muslim society, as well as in a society based on kinship or clan relations.

However, when the Soviet regime was established and the Communist ideology became dominant, freedom of expression, especially in politics, were completely liquidated. The collectivist attitudes 'duplicating' a hypertrophied allegiance to the community were combined with a full rejection of individualism.

After three or four years of Gorbachev's *perestroika* the process of democratisation of Central Asian society was forcibly imposed on the ruling establishment of the region and hardly intelligible to the overwhelming majority of its population. This can be explained again by both the general inertia of traditional society and the 'Soviet heritage', which rejected any democratic idea as soon as it appeared. Secular organisations and movements emerged in the late 1980s and early 1990s, most notably the Birlik in Uzbekistan, Rastokhez and the Democratic party in Tajikistan, Zheltoqsan in Kazakhstan and Asaba in Kirghizstan. However they had no mass base, and their character was cultural, educational or ecological from the very start.[2] At the same time, the Central Asian democrats, just like their Moscow colleagues, advocated perfection of socialism in the first months of their activities, combining that slogan with the idea of national and religious renaissance.

Initially these appeals were quite in tune with the official ideology of the Soviet Central Asian republics, whose leaders were already trying on 'nationalist garments', first cautiously and then with growing self-confidence. Besides, the so-called Islamic renaissance was becoming an important force in the region's socio-political and cultural life. The attitude of the establishment was initially rather ambivalent. On the one side, the idea of a renaissance of the religious traditions had long been in the air, and the ruling circles were ready to support it, especially since religion had been 'rehabilitated' a couple of years earlier in the Slav and Baltic republics of the USSR. The Orthodox confession in Russia and Ukraine, not to mention Lithuanian Catholicism, not only openly claimed its former role of a pastor of souls, but increasingly engaged in political activity. These developments prompted the Muslim clergy and ordinary Muslims to ask themselves why Islam was still deprived of similar opportunities.

Meanwhile the local administration, particularly at the area and district levels, were afraid of a renaissance of Islam. They were particularly anxious about the clergy's underground activities and those of the circles and 'clubs' for religious education, which appeared in the late 1980s. Besides, it was already clear that the ideas of Islamic fundamentalism enjoyed considerable popularity in the society.

The authorities' ambivalent approach to the Islamic renaissance is illustrated, in particular, by the fact that in June 1991, when the process of Islamic renaissance was already irreversible, the ideological commission of the Central Committee of the Communist Party of Uzbekistan discussed the question of atheistic (i.e. anti-Islamic) activities in several areas and adopted a special resolution 'On the religious situation in the Ferghana valley.'[3]

As a whole, the ruling circles had to reconcile themselves to the activities of the opposition forces, or 'informals' as they were referred to in the *perestroika* period. Moscow's policy of encouraging moderate opposition was among the factors that compelled them to do so. Another factor of considerable importance was the fact that the authorities perceived no serious danger in the activities of the local secular national democratic organisations.

The situation began to change after the collapse of the USSR in late 1991 and the formation of independent states in the place of Soviet socialist republics. One may assert with certain reservations that the abortive Communist coup of August 1991 in Moscow signified the end of the Central Asian democrats' and the ruling establishments' honeymoon. Becoming formally independent of Moscow, the local authorities were no longer accountable to them for the 'successful development of democracy'. As for themselves, they felt no particular need for an institutionalised opposition.

As for the lower strata of the society, they had become preoccupied more by the poor conditions of their everyday lives, inflation and deteriorating living standards than by the problems of democracy and human rights, which are a complete abstraction to the majority of the Central Asian population, especially in Uzbekistan and Tajikistan, where the authorities skilfully manipulated public opinion by emphasising the problems which democracy had brought to Russia.

To be sure, the society's and the authorities' attitudes to democracy had specific features in each state. For example in Kirghizstan, President Akaev made efforts from the very start to consolidate the institutions of democracy in his state. But even there democratic processes had been hampered by the conditions of the traditional society with its priority of tribal and clan interests. Certain changes have occurred in Kazakhstan, too, whose president Nursultan Nazarbaev is ready to 'tolerate' the opposition, while putting all possible efforts into debarring his real and potential political antagonists from access to the levers of power. The most negative attitude to the opposition is demonstrated by the ruling circles of Turkmenistan, Tajikistan and Uzbekistan.

We are not going to discuss the purely political aspect of the suppression of the opposition in these states, though that theme by itself deserves a separate study, surprisingly resembling the history of the Soviet KGB's struggle against the dissidents.

We should like to draw attention to an entirely different circumstance, namely to the manner in which the ruling class of post-Soviet Central Asia and the ideologists at their service appeal to the values of the traditional society, legitimizing the rejection of democratic values and promoting the idea of traditional social consent.

It has to be admitted that the arguments of Central Asian politicians and scholars concerning the limited application of European-style democracy in the region have substantial grounds. B. A. Abdurazzakov, an Uzbek scholar, has put it that, 'It would hardly be reasonable to approach the democratic process in our country with the yardsticks of the American reality or modern European criteria'. He holds that 'there is no united democratic space in the former Soviet Union.'[4]

Rahmon Karimov and Rawshan Okhunov of Uzbekistan express their opinion even more definitely: 'The principle of Western democracy ('I do what I want as far as it is within the framework of law') is individual oriented, and in our conditions it will inevitably clash with the interests of various groups (kin, clan, *mahalla* [urban quarter - A.M.], community, etc.), for these interests do not, naturally, invariably coincide; instead of a polyphony of individualities (Western democracy), contradictions and collisions will emerge between various groups and strata of the motley and mosaic East'.[5]

The ruling classes of Central Asia strive to compensate for the rejection of European-style democracy by an appeal to the traditions of the indigenous civilisation and to the historically formed standards of people's socio-political allegiance in traditional society. The experience of Turkmenistan, for instance, is demonstrative. Here Saparmurat Niyazov, a highly authoritative ruler, has set up a People's Council under himself with sixty representatives of all districts. This may be considered as analogous to a tribal assembly or *shura*, a council of a Muslim community. That council with consultative functions has been created to cooperate with the *mejlis*, the Turkmenian parliament. According to its chairman Sahat Muradov, it 'will become an element of democratic control over the President's activities'.[6] There was, incidentally, talk about setting up a body similar to a *shura* in Tajikistan in 1991–92. It is arguable that a council of that kind could have been a factor promoting stability in the events which led to a civil war in 1992.

However, while convening, or talking about convening, representative bodies, based on the local tradition, none of the Central Asian presidents intended to delegate any real authority to them or endow them with the right of decision making. The People's Council of Turkmenistan had purely consultative functions and did not influence the rigid authoritarian system in any way. Perhaps, in this specific case the People's Council and similar bodies at lower levels may be compared with the people's congresses in the Libyan Jamahiriya, where a political system was set up in the 1970s, also based on the principle of communal 'people's power'.

From the viewpoint of its ethno-social structure Turkmen society is very similar to that of Libya, the latter also being a conglomerate of tribes. There are analogies also in the economic structure –natural gas plays roughly the same role in the Turkmenian economy as petroleum does in Libya. Therefore, it seems more than merely symbolical that Muammar Qadhafi, the leader of the Libyan revolution, has demonstrated a special interest in Turkmenistan. Turkmen was the first language of Central Asia into which his *Green Book* was translated. A copy was presented to President Niyazov at a function in 1991.[7]

However, while creation of traditional consultative bodies under charismatic presidents is only to be expected in the Central Asian states (of course, with the exception of Turkmenistan), a no less traditional form of power also functions for instance in Uzbekistan. This is the *mahalla* council, whose informal activities continued in many places throughout the period of Soviet power.

Mahalla is the community of an urban neighbourhood, small town or village. It is the most stable social grouping and has survived numerous social upheavals within its long history, including the revolution of 1917. The *mahalla* committees always consisted of the most respected people of the neighbourhood, among whom mullahs, imams and generally the people who were literate and well versed in religion and in the reciting and interpretation of the Qur'an played a special role. These committees are effective and influential administrative bodies, with whose opinion all state power has to reckon.

Soviet power tried to ignore the *mahalla* committee, though ultimately it was compelled to take their opinion into account. Finally it not only recognised their immense influence, but tried to strengthen its influence within them and even to put them under its control. At the very beginning of the 1990s the administration attempted a virtual merger of the official bodies of representative power (the soviets of people's deputies) and *mahalla* committees. In some districts of the Ferghana area and some other areas of Uzbekistan secretaries of *mahalla* committees were paid a state salary.

Phrases like 'Communists must work in *mahallas*' began to appear in the official press. According to K. Khalitov, a high ranking official of the Ferghana area, a 'qualitatively new period' had begun in the *mahalla* committees' activities, and they were becoming 'a notable factor in the local soviets' work'.[8]

It was hoped that merger or at least interaction of the Soviet and traditional institutions of power would ensure the stability of regimes disorientated by perestroika and the changes that were occurring in the life of the country. The authorities were seeking all opportunities to maintain their influence. That trend continued after the Central Asian states became independent. The official authorities increasingly identified themselves with the traditional mode of rule. Even the names of state and municipal offices were changed to the traditional terms. For instance, the heads of city administrations came to be referred to as *hakims* in Kirghizstan and *hokims* in Uzbekistan (both words mean 'ruler'). The presidents of the new Muslim republics took their oaths by placing their hands on the Qur'an. The list of formal 'retraditionalisation' of the administrative system goes on and on.

Behind the veneer of traditional attributes, which may be considered to a certain degree to be tactical steps on the part of the ruling circles, one can find a deeper phenomenon of acquiring more natural national and religious forms of power.

It was inevitable that democracy was allotted a very insignificant space in the system of traditional political values. This is particularly clear from the local leaders' repeated statements on the need for political stability and inter-ethnic harmony (although it should be mentioned that the word 'democracy' was used extensively in the 1990s both in the Central Asian leaders' speeches and in the local press).

At the same time, while reviving the historical forms and notions related to people's power, the ruling strata of Central Asian society tried to lend a modern 'democratic' appearance to the political system. In all Central Asian states (with the exception of Turkmenistan) the principle of a multi-party system is formally recognised. In 1991 all underground or semi-underground political parties were legalised. Presidential elections with alternative candidates were held in Uzbekistan. The struggle for the presidential office in Tajikistan was hotly contested: Rahmon Nabiev, the leader of the 'old' post-Communist forces, faced Dawlet Khudonazarov, a renowned Tajik intellectual and film producer.

The authorities of Uzbekistan and Kazakhstan tried to improve relations with their political opponents, striving to make them a puppet opposition. In Uzbekistan the role of the 'pocket opposition' was allotted in 1992 to the Erk party, whose chairman Muhammad Salih was Islam Karimov's formal rival during the presidential elections (Salih's real name is Salai Madaminov a renowned writer and poet, translator of French poetry and of Franz Kafka). The Erk cooperated for some months with the ruling People's Democratic Party of Uzbekistan founded by Karimov most notably at the level of provincial administration. Bakhtiyar Rahmaev, a provincial leader of the PDPU, wrote: 'Many provisions of Erk's programme are in tune with that of the PDPU.'[9] Nursultan Nazarbaev, the president of Kazakhstan, adopted similar tactics towards the moderate opposition and managed to 'tame' the People's Congress of Kazakhstan, a notable opposition force.

The authorities' attempt to manipulate the opposition for 'demonstrative effect', and thus favourably influence the potential economic and financial donors from Europe and the USA, is combined with an onslaught, reinforced in 1993, upon the genuine opposition, who refused to partake in the facade of democracy and instead advocated radical (not always based on persuasive arguments) nationalist or national-democratic positions. The Birlik was routed in Uzbekistan, the Zheltoqsan, a radical organisation, was banned in Kazakhstan. Even in Kirghizstan the radical opposition experiences a certain pressure in the form of permanent official criticism of the Asaba, a small but popular party. As for Turkmenistan, it was described at a press conference of human rights activists in Moscow as 'the country of universal silence'. There is not even a shadow of a 'normal' opposition there.

In Tajikistan the fate of democracy was similar. The united opposition front of the Democratic Party of Tajikistan, the Islamic Renaissance Party (IRP), Rastokhez and the Lali Badakhshon organisation, in spite of the defeat in the presidential elections of 1991, became a real independent political force and was able to obtain some posts in the government in the spring of 1992. However, the opposition failed to retain power, and its short spell in the cabinet became a prologue to a bloody civil war. Sangak Safarov, the head of armed squads in the Kulab area and one of the most consistent adversaries of the opposition coalition, promised frankly to 'clear Tajikistan and Russia of the democratic wretches'.[10]

The ruling elite's offensive upon opposition forces, its persistent attempts to portray democracy as something alien to traditional values is accepted by the majority of the population, who prefer firm leadership and are often predisposed to authoritarian rule. It is interesting to note that it is not a secret to the democrats themselves, who belong to the westernised, though 'in the Soviet manner', local intelligentsia. The author had opportunities to talk with the leading members of the Birlik of Uzbekistan, the Rastokhez of Tajikistan, etc., who frankly admitted that the Central Asian democrats have almost no chances of winning a broad social base in the coming years.

Thus, Central Asian society is doubly unprepared to adopt European-style democratic values: firstly, objective reasons, i.e. the confessional and national specificity of its historical and cultural development and, secondly, because essentially the Communist regimes persist there.

In their turn, the democrats who act in the heart of traditional society also differ from their colleagues in the West. Even those of them who were brought up in a Europeanised milieu, know Russian perfectly and work as professionals outside the traditional economic sector are not free of the influence of the traditional Islamic and national mentality and are often guided by traditional standards of behaviour. On many occasions Central Asian democrats rely on family and clan relations and informal regional 'associations' and are compelled to observe the interests of a family, a clan or a compatriot community in this or that way. Examples of this kind of political party are the Birlik of Uzbekistan, headed from the very start by two brothers, Abduwahhop and Abdumannop Pulatovs, the Alash National Freedom Party of Kazakhstan, whose activities were initiated by the family of its chairman Aron Atabek, and the Democratic Party of Tajikistan, which relies mainly on the southern regions of the country.

However, the Central Asian democrats can hardly be blamed for their use of traditional connections. Firstly, it is understandable and inevitable due to the historical structures that have formed in the region. Secondly, the post-Communist structures that oppose them also use the 'old' kinship and clan ties very successfully. Political life in Central Asia cannot be severed from the context of traditional ties, of the habitual and age-long standards of relations between people, which dominate all aspects of political life.

In the absence of democratic traditions and the dominance of traditionalism in both the political and personal spheres, the prominence of Islam in the political struggle has become a stable and, perhaps, the most regular feature of the social situation in Central Asia. Almost all political forces of Central Asia appeal today to Islam: ex-Communists, national democrats, nationalists and most notably Islamic fundamentalists since 1989.

The phenomenon of Islamic fundamentalism itself is far from being simple. Most political scientists in Europe, the USA, and Russia, are negative about it. They deem it impermissible to use religion in politics, to create religious-political organisations and so on. Besides, they identify Islamic fundamentalism by and large with political extremism. In doing so, they ignore the fact that Islam is historically a politicised religion and that religion and politics remain closely interrelated in the Muslim civilisation. The level of secularisation in Muslim countries is far lower than in Christian society, and an orientation towards theocratic or quasi-theocratic authoritarianism is often discernible in their state structures. Obviously, it is Islamic fundamentalism that reflects most consistently and uncompromisingly the specific features of Islamic civilisation, which makes it distinct from Christian civilisation. Lastly, in our opinion, the most important thing is that, in expressing the 'Islamic alternative' to the Euro–Christian socio-political and economic development , the ideologists and politicians of Islamic fundamentalism try to offer an optimum model of an Islamic state in accordance with the normative principles of Islamic civilisation.

It is not our purpose to discuss whether the creation of that model is realistic . But even if we accept that the ideal is unattainable, we cannot deny that the idea of an Islamic state has millions of followers.

All this bears relevance to Central Asia, where Islamic fundamentalism is among the most active political forces and increasingly influences the political situation. Political freedom within the framework of Muslim society permits the existence of a religious-political movement, such as fundamentalism.

The socio-political basis of the emergence of a movement of that kind took shape in Central Asia, first of all in Uzbekistan and Tajikistan, as early as in the mid-1980s. However, an indisputable impetus to its spread was the setting up of branches of the Islamic Renaissance Party in the then Soviet Socialist Republics of the region.

The All-Union IRP was founded at a constituent congress held in the Russian city of Astrakhan in June 1990. Initially the backbone of the IRP was formed by the Tatar Muslims of Moscow and people from Daghestan, an autonomous republic within the Russian Federation in Northern Caucasia. Delegates from Tajikistan were also present at the congress. In the IRP leaders' opinion, its main tasks included the renaissance of Islam, the involvement of Muslims in politics and the creation of favourable conditions for adoption of the 'Islamic way of life' by every Muslim of the then USSR.[11] In the same year the committee of the IRP was registered in Moscow.

The party leaders, particularly many members of the Council of *Ulema*, its highest body, did not conceal their sympathies for Islamic fundamentalism and expressed them at the press conferences conducted by the IRP. At the same time Ahmedqadi Akhtaev, the chairman of the IRP and Wali-Ahmed Sadur, its press secretary and chief ideologist, stressed that they heavily opposed extremism and wished to act within the framework of the constitution.

In the first months of its existence the IRP was a largely insignificant vehicle of political education, little known even in the Muslim community. The situation changed after two regional conferences of the IRP were held in Dushanbe (October 1990) and Tashkent (January 1991). The party's regional branches were set up in the respective republics and became the nucleus of the fundamentalist forces. It was approximately in the same period that the Adolat (Justice), a movement for social justice, emerged in the Ferghana valley of Uzbekistan. Its members styled themselves on the Muslim Brothers and other Islamist organisation of the Arab countries of the Middle East.

The regional branches of the IRP, which were formed also in Kazakhstan and Kirghizstan, were not registered officially and acted underground.[12] After the Central Asian states were proclaimed independent and the party's regional branches became national parties under the old name of the IRP, the ban remained in effect. It was only in Tajikistan that the party was legalised on the eve of the presidential elections as a result of a prolonged struggle. However, it was banned again, when the civil war began in 1992.

The governments of the Central Asian states regarded their prohibition of activities of the IRP and other Islamist groups as a necessary measure to strengthen democracy. The official propaganda asserts that these essentially fundamentalist organisations are the arch enemies of democracy and their activities are a source of instability.

This view is debatable especially as there were occasions when it was pro-fundamentalist imams and mullahs who held back Muslim crowds from riots and preached tolerance. At the same time, occasions are known, too, when fundamentalists of a radical brand appealed for the 'liberation' of Muslim territories from 'infidels'. One thing is indisputable: the Central Asian rulers soon realised that their main rival in the struggle for power was Islamic fundamentalism rather than the uncoordinated democrats. The paradox is that in the setting of the Muslim society, where Islam has been politicised from time immemorial, persecution of fundamentalists (unless they are extremists) is antidemocratic, irrespective of the persecutors' intentions. The activities of fundamentalist organisations are an inevitable feature of the political process in Muslim countries. This is an important distinction between democracy in the Muslim East and that in the European West.

However, another question arises – how do the fundamentalists of the Muslim regions of the ex-USSR regard democracy and what do they imply in this notion? The answer is a complex one: two trends have emerged among those who hold that Islam and politics are inseparable. The supporters of the radical trend deny outright the adoption of the norms of European democracy in Muslim society. For instance, this was the position of a part of the leadership of the All-Union IRP. *Al-Wahdat*, the party's mouthpiece, carried a verbose article in 1991 under the meaningful heading 'Democracy for democrats, Islam for Muslims'. Its author argued that European democracy is incompatible with the traditions of political life in the Muslim East.[13] The most consistent supporter of this viewpoint is Geidar Jemal, a member of the IRP leadership and chairman of the Tawhid Islamic centre, who completely rejected democracy in its European interpretation. He wrote that it is Islam alone that 'ensures legal opportunities to everybody without distinction of language, nationality, skin colour, etc.'[14]

Interpretations of this kind are in tune with the position of Imam Khomeini or, say, Abu A'la al-Maududi of Pakistan, one of the most prominent ideologists of Islamic fundamentalism, who rejects democracy and the right of the majority to legislate. However, there are other fundamentalists' attitudes to democracy.

Many moderate fundamentalists, including those from among the leadership of the Islamic parties, repeatedly stated that a synthesis is possible of the Islamic political standards and modern democratic principles. Characteristically enough, talking about the prospect of the creation of an Islamic state, the Islamic leaders of Tajikistan have repeatedly stressed that this is an unrealistic goal. Most Muslims are not adequately prepared to perceive a state of this kind, and, significantly, the advance towards it must be achieved in parliamentary forms. The IRP leader Muhammadsharif Himmatzoda, his deputy Dawlat Usmon and the then Qazi-Kalon (spiritual leader) of Tajikistan

Akbar Turajonzoda all agreed on this matter.[15]

Aron Atabek, the leader of the Alash party of Kazakhstan, has also expressed his allegiance to western-style democracy. The three components of the Alash slogan are Islam, Turkicism and democracy. This slogan appeared on the front page of *Al-Haq*, the party's mouthpiece, in 1991–92.[16] Aron Atabek favours a combination of Islamic fundamentalism and European democracy. To sum up, some Islamic fundamentalists are more receptive to democratic values in politics than the present secular rulers of the Central Asian states.

The question of the possibility of mutual adaptation of western democracy and traditional Muslim society is essentially an 'eternal' question. Hopes, perhaps unrealistic, have appeared in different Muslim countries at different stages of their modern history that this synthesis was about to become a reality. But, as a rule, the traditional political culture, based on Islam, has proved stronger, and democracy has had to retreat or compromise.

It is very difficult to predict how well democracy has taken root in the Muslim societies of Central Asia which have survived totalitarianism. The first democratic experiments failed tragically almost everywhere. A feature of the Central Asian situation is that timid attempts to plant the seeds of democracy are made against the background of a burgeoning Islamist movement. The occasions are not rare when the two forces, though very different, cooperate in resisting post-Communist authoritarianism. It may become clear in the near future how this will affect the development of democracy in Central Asia and how democracy, in its turn, will influence Islamic fundamentalism.

Notes

1. For details see: S. P. Polyakov. *Traditsionalizm v sovremennom sredneaziatskom obshchestve* (Traditionalism in the modern Central Asian society). Znanie, Moscow, 1989.

2. See, for instance, the constitution and programme of the Rastokhez in the organisation's mouthpiece: *Rastokhez*, No 5, November 1990; and 'The programme of the movement in defence of nature, spiritual values and material wealth of Uzbekistan' (a MS in the author's archives). Birlik, the name of the movement, means unity.

3. *Pravda Vostoka* (Tashkent), June 7, 1991.

4. *Narodnoe Slovo* (Tashkent), January 11, 1992.

5. *Pravda* (Moscow), July 14, 1993. It is significant that the reasoning

about the unsuitability of European democracy to Asian society appeared in the very Communist mouthpiece that regularly convinces its readers that democracy is alien to Russian society, too.

6. *Nezavisimaya Gazeta* (Moscow), December 12, 1992.
7. *Turkmenskaya Iskra* (Ashkhabad), December 27, 1991.
8. *Narodnoe Slovo*, February 19, 1992.
9. *Sovetskaya Bukhara* (Bukhara), February 27, 1992.
10. *Nezavisimaya Gazeta*, December 5, 1992.
11. For details see: *Programma i ustav Islamkoy partii vozrozhdeniya* (The programme and constitution of the Islamic Renaissance Party). Moscow, 1990.
12. As for Turkmenistan, the local security bodies managed to hinder the convening of the IRP's conference. There was no party branch there. At the same time, according to the IRP leadership, in 1991 several dozen Turkmenian citizens considered themselves party members.
13. *Al-Wahdat* (Moscow), March, 1991.
14. *Den* (Moscow), October 25 to November 8, 1991.
15. See, for instance, *Narodnaya Gazeta* (Dushanbe), June 19, 1992; *Izvestiya* (Moscow), May 13, 1992; *Adolat* (Dusanbe), No 5, 1991, etc.
16. See *Al-Haq*, November 1991, Alma-Ata.

5

Islam in Tatar National Ideology and Policy

R. M. Amirkhanov

The national liberation movement of a people creates its own national ideology which, in the process of moving towards independence, is opposed to an imperial chauvinist ideology. A national ideology is based on the historical path taken by a people as well as on its spiritual experience as seen through the prism of the final objectives of national struggle. A national ideology is a concept with many aspects to be understood and interpreted, but the spiritual elements are the essence of the national idea in the process of achieving national independence and the right to self-determination.

The achievement of this objective is connected with a process of spiritual emancipation and revival of the nation, and with the realisation by the nation of its historic uniqueness. The thinkers of the 'New Time', the time of the Tatar revival beginning with Marjani saw that spiritual emancipation and originality of thought were the basic conditions of renewal and progress. If we turn to the national ideology of Tatars three fundamental spiritual principles are to be singled out. They are: Islamism, Turkism and Tatar nationalism by which we mean a mature politicised form of the public self-consciousness of the nation. Before we proceed to the analysis proper of the role of Islam in the formation of national ideology and policy, we need a general characterisation of these three principles in the context of the development of Tatar public thought.

First, what do we mean by Islamism? More than a thousand years have passed since Islam came to the Tatar people.[1] During this time Islam has so deeply permeated their life, their consciousness and outlook that it is impossible to imagine the place of the Tatars in world civilisation outside the Muslim world and its civilisation.

The place of Islam at various periods of Tatar history differed or, rather, different aspects of Islam came into focus in the Muslim community depending on the particular conditions pertaining. In the epoch of forced conversion to Christianity (from the mid-16th until the end of the 18th century), Islam was a means by which Tatars preserved their historical identity, it became the ideology of an anti-colonial national liberation struggle. The reforms of the government of Catherine II at the end of the 18th century conceded the failure of the imperial policy of the extermination of Islam[2] and a new chapter in the history of the Tatar people. In public thought since then those aspects of Islamic teaching that have encouraged progress have come to the fore. The most important functions of Islam in the national ideology at the present time are as follows. Islam is filling the vacuum created by the collapse of Communism, returning to the people its trust in genuine values bringing up a generation which thinks and believes in basic humanitarian principles. The fate of our people will depend on the ability of the new generation to use the historic opportunity and to bring to a conclusion the struggle for national rights.

The second fundamental basis of the national ideology is Turkism. As an ideology, as a weapon of the national liberation struggle of the Turkic peoples Turkism is a relatively new phenomenon. But from the point of view of spiritual and ethnic kinship and of a common historical fate, the roots of Turkism go back centuries. This feeling of kinship has never deserted the Turks. No wonder that the related peoples count in the first instance on each other in their struggle for equal rights and opportunities of development. Today, at a time of the establishment and strengthening of national Turkic states, the union and solidarity of these peoples around common interests and aims are especially evident. The Turkic world with its history, material and spiritual culture shares a set of common problems. The Tatar people are an indispensable part of the all-Turkic civilisation. Therefore the Tatar national ideology includes common Turkic political and cultural priorities, and the Tatar national movement considers it a moral obligation to give help and political support to the struggle of all Turkic peoples for their national rights.

Finally, the third spiritual basis of a national ideology is nationalism. This we need to dwell on in more detail. If the first two principles, Islamism and Turkism, characterise the Tatars as part of the whole (the Muslim and Turkic worlds respectively), nationalism is a historical category reflecting the nation as a separate unique world. Nationalism involves, from a philosophical-historical point of view, in our opinion, the emergence of a national identity marking the evolution of people into a nation, into a historic community, which realises its historicity, its 'separateness' as a full social organism of the world community of nations.

Secondly, the essence of nationalism during 75 years of Bolshevism was so distorted that even today we take the words 'nationalism', 'nationalist' as an accusation. The propaganda of the dominant power used its centuries of experience and all the might of the state apparatus to create an image of the nationalist as the internal enemy. As a result of such long persecution of nationalists, even today when public opinion is slowly being freed from the cast-iron stereotypes of imperial propaganda, nationalism is still a source of fear for the average Russian, it is still a source of all evil for the apologists of a 'whole and indivisible' power.

It would not be so sad if this 'imperial' interpretation of nationalism came only from the dominant ideologists. Unfortunately, a considerable part of our own national intelligentsia, among them many scholars who are seeking truly to serve their people, are still under the influence of the dominant critique of this ideology in their attitude to nationalism. We need now our own criteria for the evaluation of our history, culture, and ideology. As nationalism is not something external to the national consciousness but the result of its development, it is a superstructure of the mature form of the national self-consciousness. But plainly, if national feeling reflects one's love of one's people, language, culture, customs and traditions, then at the level of nationalism a certain bitterness is added, the bitterness of realising the humiliating reality of the public existence and a passionate desire to see one's people free and equal among equals. The essence of the idea of nationalism is the realisation of this goal.

Thus, nationalism becomes an ideological weapon of the national-liberation movements of all peoples entering the arena of independent political life. Every nation moves inescapably towards getting rid of colonial oppression and obtaining its own statehood. This ideology is an inevitable reaction of colonial peoples against the imperial ideology in the process of forming the national self-consciousness. Its subsequent disappearance is connected directly with disappearance of the cause of this ideology, namely the inequality of nations.

At the beginning of the 20th century, in the short period of the rapid development of Tatar culture, public thought, and the national liberation movement, such thinkers as G. Ishaki, F. Amirhan, and G. Tukai developed the concept of *milliyatche* (nationalist) in its primordial sense of a patriot of the nation (*milliyat*), of a man who suffers for the fate of his people and who devotes himself to the cause of serving his people and its future. National feelings, as G. Tukai put it himself, are the most sacred and hallowed, and national dreams are the brightest. It is because of their respect for the concept of *milliyat* that Tukai and his followers severely criticised pseudo-nationalists, who vulgarised the national idea in demagogy or used it for mercenary ends. From the same high standard they mercilessly unmasked the exploitation of the authority of Islam and the religious feelings of people by the bourgeoisie and ministers of religion, who 'forgot' God, religion and justice for their own benefit. The progressive thinkers saw true *milliyatche*, nationalists, in such faithful, fearless and honest sons of the nation as G. Ishaki who, according to F. Amirhan, '... both in his 'tangism'[3] and in his critique of 'nationalists' has always remained a nationalist, that is all his actions were guided by the interests of the nation.'[4]

In general, nationalism in Tatar public thought of the beginning of the 20th century had none of those feelings of superiority or hostility to other peoples which were to be attributed to it later by Soviet propaganda. Propaganda depicted nationalism, along with Islam as the main obstacle to the 'international community', which was to include the spiritual assimilation of Turkic Muslims. Nationalism was slandered, distorted and confused with chauvinism, but even Bolsheviks failed to return the nation to the 'pre-nationalist' past, failed to deprive the nation of the newly discovered feeling of national dignity. Incidentally, one of the first *olu milliyatchelerden* (great nationalists) of modern times was Sh. Marjani. This outstanding scholar understood one important thing: if Tatar self-preservation required Islam then for progress, evolution and a place under the sun national pride was also necessary. Hence the attention of this thinker was devoted to Tatar history, culture and literature. The crucial question Marjani poses to his fellow-believers from the pages of *Mustafad al-akbar fi ahvali Kazan ve Boulgar* (the main historical work by Sh. Marjani): 'if not a Tatar then who are you?'[5] Indeed, if the name Tatar, in the mouth of a chauvinist, sounds like a swear word, is this a reason to give it up?

The name of a people is not clothes which you may wear for a time and then throw away!

Certainly, there are not infrequent negative moments in the practice of a national-liberation struggle, in the confrontation of national and chauvinistic interests, in the confrontation of nationalists and chauvinists. They are often a consequence of the hatred to the enslavers, accumulated over decades and centuries, and of the bitterness of national humiliation, the bitterness of one's own inferiority among sovereign nations. But, we must stress, the essence of nationalism lies not in these negative aspects, but in the aspiration to political and legal parity among nations. This aspiration is then presented by the dominant propaganda as the pretensions of nationalists to exclusiveness and superiority, arousing enmity, etc. In other words, in order to discredit it nationalism is blamed for all the sins of its ideological opposite namely chauvinism, the inseparable companion of the imperial ideology. Thus nationalism in the epoch of Bolshevism was reduced to the level of ideological banditry. It is not by chance that the aphorism 'chauvinism is the last refuge of the scoundrel' was 'corrected' during the Soviet era by adding the word 'nationalism' at the beginning.

Today nationalism may be considered the leading ideological basis of the national ideology because it includes national aspects of Islamism and Turkism, becoming in that sense their synthesis. Maturing and hardening on the arena of political struggle, the national ideology is enriched by international experience as it perfects its own vision of national progress. Thus, by the beginning of the 20th century Tatar public political thought had in its arsenal important aspects of the democratic thought of the West (parliamentary democracy, human rights), presenting the peculiarity of the geo-political situation of the Tatar world as a link between East and West and a synthesis of progressive social teachings with the traditional Islamic values.

This process of renewal and enrichment of the national ideology by way of a degree of 'Westernisation', does not mean the weakening of its Turkic and Islamic roots. Each of the three ideological bases of the national ideology takes its own place in the whole system of the moral and spiritual values. Just try to imagine what would remain of the national idea without its Turkic or Islamic roots: they are unimaginable apart.

In the same way, in our opinion it is impossible to oppose the

national moral bases and democratic ideals. On the contrary, man
reaches the heights of human values through the deep perception of
the national idea. We Tatars learn the human ideals through the prism
of the norms of justice, equality and charity which permeate our being
and have passed down generations. However, for us in our
consciousness the triumph of these principles is conditioned in the
first analysis by national equality. Without solving the national question
on the basis of humanistic principles the beautiful ideas of democracy,
the law-based state and human rights will remain for a nationally
oppressed identity just that, beautiful but empty ideas. From the
nationalist position the key opening the door to a law-based society is
an unconditional acceptance and guarantee of the right of a nation to
self-determination. There is no other way to achieve a society of law
and human rights. This is confirmed by four centuries of experience
of European democracy as well as the inglorious fate of the Soviet
empire.

Speculations contrasting the rights of nations to human rights and
freedoms are also fruitless. Can human rights be guaranteed and
implemented without national rights? The answer is definitely no:
only together can they be realised.

The national state, a law-based society, and human rights - these
are links in the same chain. Nations pass along this road, sometimes
very painfully with retreats and losses, and they certainly move along
this road at different speeds. To the necessity of uniting into various
unions, commonwealths and confederations they will also come in
their own time by natural and historical roads in the way West
European peoples have arrived at today.

Now, let us turn our attention to a concrete historical evaluation of
the role of Islam in the formation of the national ideology of the
Tatars. In this respect, the influence and place of Islam in the thousand
year old tradition of the Tatar people, can be divided into three main
periods. The first consists of the centuries of development of the
ancestors of the modern Tatars in conditions of independent statehood
when Islam was state religion and ideology. This period, the 10th to
16th centuries, is the epoch of the Volga Bulgars, the Golden Horde
and the Kazan Khanate (until its fall in the middle of the 16th century).
According to historians the confessional situation at that time was
characterised by a relative freedom of religious cults, beliefs, by a broad
toleration by the Muslim rulers of other religions and their priests. As

documentary and literary sources show,[6] in the Turkic Volga region and the Urals the moderate and tolerant Hanafi persuasion (*madhhab*) of Islam and the moderate Sufism of the school of al-Ghazali found favourable ground. The Sufi Naqshbandi school, which did not accept extreme asceticism and estrangement from the secular life characteristic of more radical trends of Muslim mysticism, enjoyed great popularity among the Turkish Muslims of the Volga region.

The domination in the northern domains of Islam of this moderate trend is, in our opinion, down to the cultural traditions of pre-Islamic Turkic communities, and by the geo-political and historical conditions around the formation of the Turkic state in the Volga–Kama region. Indeed, since ancient times peoples of different pagan confessions lived in this region, while the Volga–Bulgar state formed in the 8th to 10th centuries strengthened and achieved wide recognition as a northern centre of international trade, economic and cultural contacts. Here Christians from Rus, Muslims from Central Asia and the Middle East, Jews from Khazaria lived, met at fairs and concluded deals with pagans from the European North. This helped in working out a broad and sober view of various religions, contributed to the promotion of tolerance among the economically most active social groups which were involved in trade and exchange. A similar attitude to religions acquired the status of state policy in the epoch of the Golden Horde, which was dictated not least by a desire to preserve political stability inside the multi-ethnic and multi-confessional state and by the significance attached to external economic relations with the Christian and Muslim world. It is common knowledge that the rights and, in the Middle Ages, unprecedented privileges accorded different confessions, their lands and their property, were preserved and guaranteed by the Khan Yarliks. These privileges provided the fertile soil for the growth of the wealth and status of the Orthodox Church, which later, at the time of the disintegration of the Golden Horde, became the uniting centre of Rus in its struggle against the power of the very Horde, which had fostered it.[7]

The religious situation in the region changed radically after the conquest of the Kazan and other Tatar Khanates in the second half of the 16th century. The Russian autocracy and the Orthodox Church unleashed a merciless struggle against the Muslims, which was aimed at the destruction of Islam. The policy of tolerance and liberty of conscience[8] gave way to a state policy of the enforced Christianisation of adherents of different faiths. The methodical destruction of mosques and Muslim books began, the Muslims were driven from their homes, and they had to pay additional taxes, while those who converted to Christianity were excused these taxes. In these conditions Islam was for Turkish Muslims the main ideological support in preserving their historic and cultural identity; it was the main method of opposing the ideological aggression of autocracy and Orthodoxy.

This aggression, increasing or weakening depending on the domestic political situation in Russia, continued for more than two hundred years until the last quarter of the 18th century. By then the reforms of the government of Catherine II had acknowledged the failure of the policy of the forced extermination of Islam and the spiritual unification of 'believers of other religions' on the basis of Orthodoxy. The national and Islamic values of the Tatars were preserved at a very high price. Adherence to the traditional way of life and self-isolation, prevented the introduction into Tatar life of progressive social-political and, scientific-technical achievements as well as the cultural ideas of Europe. The status of Sufism, as the true remedy for individual salvation in the conditions of an alien environment, increased. We see it in the creative life of the great Tatar poet of the 17th century, Mavli Kuli, whose *Hikmet*s bring to life the traditions of the Turkic poet-Sufi of the 12th century A. Yasavi. We see it in the spread of the religious-Sufi works of the medieval ages, which educated Muslims in the high moral patterns of early Islam, but which were helpless in the real problems of development in the Muslim world, which was in a state of deep stagnation.

At the same time, in this gloomy epoch, Islam also became the ideological pillar of the socially active, rebellious tendency in the struggle of Muslims against the colonial policy of Tsarism. The whole second half of the 16th century and the beginning of the 17th century were characterised by the desperate efforts of Tatars to restore their lost independence. In this unequal struggle the physical and intellectual strength of the people weakened. 'In a country where violence and terror gave way to uprising and struggle for independence,' wrote G. Iskhaki, 'it was impossible to speak about a normal economic or cultural development.'[9]

The defeat of spontaneous uprisings followed by punitive measures led to a mood of helplessness, creating a favourable ground for Sufi conceptions of individual escape by withdrawing into one's inner world, which is the last line of defence. This was the era of the 17th-century Sufi poet Mavli Kuli. The 18th century, however, brings a new wave of Muslim national-liberation movements. The Ukaz (Bill) of the Russian Senate of 1740 resulted in a new wave of forced baptism of Muslims in the Volga region, to which the latter responded with decisive resistance which in 1755 turned into an uprising under the leadership of Batirsha (Gabdulla Aliyev). Another significant revolutionary action by Muslims, which went under the slogan of revival of the Bulgar state, was the movement headed by Mullah Murat (the second half of the 1760s). Finally, in 1773–75 a peasant war headed by Y. Pugachov was unleashed, which was fervently supported by Tatars and Bashkirs. This series of riots made the government of Catherine II change their forceful tactics into a more flexible one in their struggle against Muslims. By the Ukaz on the creation in Ufa[10] of the Muslim Dukhovnoye Sobraniye (a governing body of the Muslims) the activities of mullahs are legalised, construction of mosques began and each mosque opened *medrese*s and *mektep*s.

Finally, at the third stage of its development, from the end of the 18th century until the Bolshevik revolution in 1917, Islam emerged as a banner of national revival and progress. As a result of the development of a bourgeoisie in Russia, the liberalisation of policy towards the Muslims of the Volga region, the appearance of a national bourgeoisie, the accumulation of capital, and the increase of educated people, a strata of secular intelligentsia was formed who started to plan social and national progress. The traditional way of life little by little gave way to a revision of cultural values from the point of view of the progressive transformations in the life of Muslims, which were necessary to overcome backwardness and stagnation.

Under these conditions the progressive potential of Islam as the spiritual stimulant of the social, cultural and scientific development of the Muslim community is the focus of attention of Tatar intellectuals beginning with G. Utis Imyani and G. Kursavi. In the writings of the progressives Islam is conceived as a vehicle of public and national revival. The inspiration of the epoch of the Tatar renaissance, a scholar and a poet G. Utiz Imyani (1754–1834) in his programmatic work *Muhammat az-zaman* (The Objectives of the Time, 1920) calls on his educated countrymen to give up their negative confrontation with innovation in favour of a positive cultural educational activity. A philosopher and theologian G. Kursavi (1776–1814) puts the principles of rationalism into his interpretation of the canons of Islam. His ideas were then developed by an outstanding Tatar philosopher and reformer of the 19th century Sh. Marjani (1818–89). In the second half of the 19th century the theoretical preconditions of religious reform found realisation in the ideology and practice of Jadidism. In the creative heritage and practice of the adherents of the enlightenment and the Jadids (such as Sh. Marjani, Kh. Fayezhanov, K. Nasiri, later R. Fahretdinov, M. Bigiyov, F. Karimi, S. Maksudi, etc.) the teaching of Islam appears as a spiritual pillar of an orderly, just and moral society.

At the beginning of the 20th century, in the era of the Russian revolutions, socialist ideas began to spread in Tatar society. In the creative work of the radical Tatar thinkers and public figures (G. Ishaki, F. Amirhan, G. Tukay and others) socialist teaching is combined with the ethical principles of Islam (justice, social solidarity, charity), thus acquiring the form of ethical socialism. The essence of socialism, as a young generation of Tatar intellectuals perceived it, was in the principles of freedom, justice, social and national equality, that is in its overall humanist contents. In this way socialism, a theory of Western origin, acquired through the prism of the ethical principles of Islam, joined the ideological arsenal of the national-liberation struggle and the enlightening movements among the Tatars of the beginning of the 20th century.

Thus, in the 19th and the beginning of the 20th century the teaching of Islam, re-evaluated from the standpoint of the tasks of public progress and national freedom, became the socio-ethical basis of the anti-colonial movement and its ideology.

Beginning from the second half of the 1920s Bolshevism unleashed its policy of spiritual unification and Russification under the banner of 'proletarian internationalism'. A total attack on religion and the clergy began. Under these conditions again the preserving functions of Islam came to the fore. Islam was driven to the very bottom of public life, but it remained in the sphere of personal spiritual life, from which the Bolsheviks failed to drive it.

Long before its complete collapse as a state ideology, Bolshevism was decaying while Islam was gradually returning into public life. However, the imposed breach of continuity of the cultural traditions seriously complicated this process. If we compare the modern 'Tatar Islam' with that of the beginning of this century, the comparison will clearly not be in favour of that of today. If we want to revive and strengthen the moral foundations of the nation, we need to revive the humanist and ethical values of Islam from the very depths of the national life of Tatars. This role is in the stimulating of progressive public changes, in their moral justification, in bringing up the young generation in the humanistic values of Islam and promoting its function as a moral counterpart to the excessive search for material well-being. At the same time, we think that in Tatar society there is no historical basis and no social basis for Islam to perform the function of the main pillar in the life of the state.

So, we see the place of Islam in Tatar national life and ideology firstly, as a basis of national identity, customs and traditions and of moral upbringing. Secondly as a spiritual inspiration of public life based on the humanistic values enshrined by Islam. The realisation of the first task depends a lot on the men of religion (*ruhanilar*), while the realisation of the second task depends on the secular intelligentsia (*ziyalilar*).

In the light of the above approach to the problem of 'Islam and the National Ideology' one can try to assess some of the theoretical aspects of modern political processes in Tatar society. These are connected with the present struggle of the Tatar people for national independence and state sovereignty of the Republic of Tatarstan. First and foremost, viewed from the position of the national ideology, the realisation of the internationally accepted right of the nation to self-determination is the highest essence of the struggle for the sovereignty of the Republic of Tatarstan (representing the Tatar nation). There is no other way to ethnic and cultural survival, to growth and progress but the realisation of this right in the form of a reconstruction of the sovereign state. This is because the sovereign state alone is a necessary condition and a sure guarantee of full national development. The national ideology gives priority to the spiritual side of the achievement of the sovereignty, which in its turn will favourably influence the material well-being of all the citizens.

Through the prism of the national ideology we would like to clarify the correlation of the notions of national and state sovereignty. In our understanding the concept of self-determination, of sovereignty does not apply to the whole population (or the people) of the Republic of Tatarstan, but to the Tatar people and the Tatar nation. This is not only because Tatarstan is, for Tatars, the historic motherland. The point is that in this republic only the Tatars represent national integrity.

Therefore the sovereignty of the Tatar nation is the basis of the state sovereignty of the Republic of Tatarstan. On the other hand, national sovereignty functioning in the form of state sovereignty legalises the equality of all the citizens and ensures its international legitimacy.

If we admit that the population of this or that territory is the prime subject of sovereignty, we reduce a national republic to the level of a region or some other administrative-territorial unit. In every such region, in every such district, there would be a 'multinational people' which would be absurd. In such a case, firstly, the historical criterion would be lost. Secondly, the administrative-territorial units of the former Soviet empire, including the modern borders of Tatarstan, were defined absolutely arbitrarily; they appeared, changed, reappeared at the will of the former officers of the Kremlin. Such arbitrary formations do not coincide with national entities formed by natural historical processes.[11]

By the logic of the present Kremlin strategists, embodied in the new constitution of Russia, Tatarstan, as well as the other national republics, is given a status at the same level as other Russian districts. Thus the Tatars and other non-Russian peoples are again placed by 'democratic' Russia in the epoch of the colonial autocracy, being deprived of even the right to self-determination proclaimed by the Bolsheviks. The idea of 'equating' rights of a whole (the nation) with the parts of a whole (administrative territories) displays the clearly defined unitarian character of the state structure of Russia, covered by the fig-leaf of federalism. The new constitution (which was not accepted by Tatarstan) totally ignores the obligations of Russia to observe the international pacts guaranteeing the right of nations to self-determination.

The sovereignty of the Tatar nation, realising itself in the form of the state sovereignty of Tatarstan, ensures through the constitution equal rights and possibilities for all its citizens in all spheres of the public life. But the strategic aim of the Republic of Tatarstan, the very essence of its formation and function (in the light of the national idea) lies in the revival and development of the Tatar nation, in returning to Tatars the feeling of national value and national pride. And this in its turn demands the working out of a national outlook, of the national criteria of assessment of the historical process and the place in it of one's own people, which presents the conceptual basis of the national ideology. In present-day Tatarstan this ideology exists and develops spontaneously, at an amateur level, by the efforts of representatives of the national movements

On the state level the internationalist ideology behind the fine rhetoric of friendship between the peoples of Tatarstan still reigns and the status quo of greater Russian rule is unchanged. This state ideology will for some time help the present leadership in retaining the loyal image of Tatarstan in relation to Russia. But from the point of view of winning real sovereignty for the republic, based on the sovereignty of the nation, this ideology has no future. In the struggle for real sovereignty the state needs a spiritual pivot, uniting the nation into a whole through national aims. Granted, Tatarstan is a multi-ethnic republic, but it is also a national republic in the sense that it is the motherland of the Tatar nation, in which people of many other nations live. Therefore positive support for a civil society in Tatarstan must be accompanied by a state policy prioritising the revival of the Tatar nation, because only in Tatarstan is such a policy possible.

Without a national idea and a national aim, Tatarstan will be seen by the world community as a separatist-minded administrative territory of Russia, which is how it is presented by the Moscow politicians. Animated by the national idea, united by the national aim, in the face of all external and internal obstacles on the way to this aim, Tatarstan declares itself to be a historically determined and legitimate sovereign national state.

A few words by way of conclusion of this topic. The Turkic world occupies in geographical, historical and cultural respects a middle place between the classical East and the West, combining both Oriental and Western elements. In global politics, too, it can serve as a linking and stabilising factor between the East and the West, and thus escape being the target of the strategic interests of the world powers. The Tatars, northern Turks on the whole, have occupied in their turn a middle position in the Turkic world, since the time when the Bulgar state was a link between the European and Asian Turks. Present day Tatarstan also occupies a political position bridging the sovereign Turkic peoples (such as Turkey, Azerbaidjan, and Uzbekistan) and the Turkic peoples deprived of any form of statehood (the Crimean Tatars, Kumirs, Nogais and others). Therefore, the political future of one of the great Turkic peoples, the Tatars, will, in our opinion, reflect the tendency of the development of the whole Turkic world, brought about by the collapse of the Soviet empire. Tatarstan can and should again acquire its historical role as a bridge between the Turkic and the Euro-Asian world. However this is a question of the priorities of state policy, which should not be equated with the national ideology, though in no case should they be in contradiction with each other. The state ideology is wider than the national one, as the internal and external policies based on it are defined by many other factors besides the national one. These factors are: the ethnic composition of the population, the co-existence of the two main traditional confessional groups, relations with Russia, relations with the Tatars living outside the territory of modern Tatarstan and making up the major part of the Tatar people, and many other factors constituting the sphere of the state interests of the republic. But bearing in mind the future of the Tatar nation, we think the Tatar national idea should be founded on the basis of Tatarstan's ideology. Only on such a basis will Tatarstan realise the right to self-determination and become a guarantor of the preservation and development of the Tatar people as a full member of the world family of nations.

On the threshold of the 21st century, when many peoples of the former USSR have come close to the critical point at which an irreversible process of national degeneration begins (and many smaller peoples have, alas, crossed this line), the problem of national revival is universal as each such loss impoverishes the world we live in. In this sense all peoples and their national liberation movements have a right to expect from the world community, from its official and public structures, political and moral support and admission of their right to a free and independent choice of their path of development, which is the true criterion of democracy in a multi-national country.

Notes

1.   In 1989 a conference was held in Kazan devoted to the 1100th anniversary (according to the hijra) of the adoption of Islam by the Volga Bulgar state in 922, the year of the arrival of an embassy from the Baghdad Caliphate. At the conference some participants argued for a much earlier penetration of Islam into the Volga region (8th century).

2.   In 1782 in Kazan a Tatar town hall was opened. In 1787 by the decree of Catherine II the privileges were returned to some Tatar *murzas* - the gentility, and in 1789 in Ufa a *Duhovnoye Upravleniye* (Management) of the Muslims of Russia was formed.

3.   The term comes from the name of the newspaper *Tang Yoldizi* (The

Morning Star), around which during the years of the first Russian revolution (1905–7) the Tatar SRs (social-revolutionaries) joined, headed by G. Ishaki.

4.   Fateh Amirhan. *Eserler*. Durt Tomda. T.3., Kazan, 1989, 306 b.

5.   Sh. Marjani. *Mustafad al-akbar fi ahvali Kazan ve Boulgar*. Kazan, 1989, p. 44.

6.   So, Ibn Fadlan in his 'Notes' about the travel of the Baghdad embassy to the Volga in 922 spoke about the prevalence of the Hanafi *madhhab* among the Volga Bulgars. A modern scholar, E. A. Khalikova, comes to the same conclusion in her book 'The Muslim Necropolis of the Volga Bulgars of the 10th to early 13th centuries' based on the analysis of the archaeological materials. The great Bulgar-Tatar poet and thinker Kul Gali (13th century) in particular singles out the founder of the Hanafi *madhhab*, Abu Hanifa, in his poem *Kissai Yusuf*.

7.   Richard Pipes notes in this connection that: 'The golden age of Orthodoxy in Russia coincided with Tatar power. The Tatars liberated all the clergy from the duties, which had been imposed on all the enslaved population by the Yasa of Chingiz Khan. They gave the Orthodox Church protection and liberation from the tributes in return for a promise to pray for the Khan and his family' (Richard Pipes. 'The Church and Religion', *Nezavisimaya Gazeta*, 1993, N 111).

8.   A Russian historian of the Soviet period Khudyakov considers the tolerance typical for the Kazan Khanate to be one 'of the brightest sides' of its public life (M. G. Khudyakov. *Essays on the History of the Kazan Khanate*, Moscow, Insan publishing House, 1991, p.198).

9.   Gayaz Iskhaki. *Idel-Ural*. Kazan. Tatar Publishing House, 1991, p. 25.

6

Islam, Christianity and New Religious Trends in Tatarstan: The Issue of Conversion

R. Baltanov and G. Baltanova

One of the characteristics of the process of religious revival in the former USSR is the growth of the number of denominations. For example, in 1987 there were six registered denominations in the Autonomous Republic of Tatarstan (Islam, Orthodoxy, Baptism, Adventism, Old Rites Church, Evangelicals). By 1993 there were more than twenty denominations, among them traditional and non-traditional (Bahaism, Krishnaism, Ahmadia, etc.).

We have to say that in our society, where within a period of only half a dozen years ideological revolutions have totally changed the spiritual climate, religious revivalism is one of the most stable, growing and interesting phenomena. Religious revivalism affects traditional religiosity as well as non-traditional. In public opinion in post-communist society, those whom we call converts are met with a variety of different responses. By converts we mean those people who came to religion at a mature age, by themselves, and whose conversion is a conscious voluntary act. The majority of the people think that their transformation is not serious, that it is the result of coincidence or even for material reasons. The articles in the mass media in Russia and Tatarstan about new religious movements or converts remind one of the atheistic propaganda of the Soviet Union.

Our deep conviction, and we will try to justify it here, is that the phenomenon of 'new converts' needs serious attention, that it has deep social, psychological and intellectual roots and reasons, that it is 'true religiosity' and even more sincere than the traditional, 'national' or 'ritual' religiosity preserved in our society during the years of 'state atheism'. But before studying this subject we must first consider the question: does religious revivalism really exist in ex-USSR?

The democratisation of relationships between state and church is one of the undoubted achievements of the reforms in post-communist society. At the end of the 1980s both Western and Russian researchers wrote of a religious renaissance affecting all religious denominations. The evidence indicates that this is true. We see the growing number of registered religious communities in all the states and republics of the CIS, we see many people in the mosques and churches. Stadiums throughout the CIS at the very beginning of the 1990s, when foreign missionaries began their activity, were crowded. The mass media, television, cinemas and literature were full of religious issues and our leaders at all levels often used the church in their politics. A positive view of religion in the history of different peoples and in their culture and civilisation prevailed. Atheistic propaganda gave way to a completely un-critical attitude to religion, even its idealisation.

But after some years the reflection of the idea of religious revivalism in social scientific literature in Russia has changed slightly. It became evident, that the expected religious explosion did not take place. Recent sociological reviews have shown that the real level of religiosity did not increase very substantially. For example, a public opinion survey by the All Russia Centre for the Study of Public Opinion in Moscow showed that the proportion of believers is about 40 per cent, which is not very different from previous indications of the level of religiosity.

The same picture is to be seen in the Republic of Tatarstan. Recent sociological analysis shows us varying results ranging from 90 per cent of Muslim believers in the population to 9-10 per cent. This divergence in the results depends on the different primary definitions: whom do we call believers? Those who believe, those who practice, those who fulfil all the obligatory demands of religion? We need to come to a workable definition of religiosity. But is such a universal criterion for different systems of faith possible - is it possible even for one of them, for Islam for example? If we take a view of Islam based on its strict system of obligations we will, of course, have quite different indicators than if we define a 'believer' based on self-identification.

This contradiction exists in modern Russian religious studies generally. For example, at a conference on religion and social conflicts in Krakow, 1993, there was a discussion among Belorussian researchers on the question of the level of religiosity in Belorussia. Some of the scientists took the position of a broader interpretation of religiosity, and they assessed the level of religiosity to be very high (near 80 per cent). But the others insisted that the definition of religiosity had not changed since the period of atheistic propaganda.

Concerning Islam in Tatarstan we can say that, from our point of view, religiosity has not changed very much, because Islam needs special knowledge and a system of upbringing, which was totally destroyed in the socialist atheistic society and is only now being slowly restored. The phenomenon which is developing in ex-Soviet republics is not yet religious revivalism in its proper meaning, it is only the beginning: we could describe it as an intensification of confessional activity. Real qualitative changes of religiosity have only just begun. So, from our point of view, the notion of a rapid rise of influence of religion on post-communist society is exaggerated.

But of course, the changes have begun, and liberty of consciousness, of religions and cults has made people free to choose to believe or not, and whom to worship. The failure of communist ideology and the disintegrative nature of the ideology of nationalism has made religion one of the most popular and popularised remedies for a decaying society.

In this situation an increasing movement in 'search of God' has begun, and the phenomenon of 'new converts' appeared. Of course, this phenomenon is not new. From the history of Tatarstan we know of many examples of campaigns of proselytism, forcible or not. For example, when the Bulgars and then the Tatars were converted to Islam (respectively in the 9th and 13th centuries) they were a significant influence in the partial Islamisation of neighbouring peoples of the Volga region: Mari, Chuvash and Udmurt. After the Tsarist colonisation a process of violent Christianisation started, continuing throughout the pre-revolutionary period, and realised in different forms through both economic and non-economic coercion.

But the modern process of changing faith has some differences. The main difference is that modern conversion is the result of individual choice rather than of policy from above or of coercion. Another is that people have a real choice, and the subordination of religions as between privileged and oppressed religions is not so strong, or perhaps not so evident, as in the past. The other distinguishing feature from the past and from, for example, modern European countries is that proselytising activity has been practically out of control and outside the law. Only now has a policy of management and regulation of religions begun, but we see that this often goes to extremes, ranging from an assault on the democratic rights of some to the granting of privileges to certain confessions.

Unfortunately, we have not found any special investigation into the problems of conversion and proselytism. As we know, in Soviet-Russian philosophy of religions there was no special research devoted to this theme. This subject is closely connected with the study of sociology of religion, which was not very well developed in Soviet human sciences. Thus for us, investigation of this subject is only at the beginning.

Secondly, we came across the problem of conversion while studying traditional religiosity - Muslim and Orthodox - in Tatarstan. Of course, we knew of examples of change of religious adherence but we had not imagined that it was so wide spread. We could not speak about a percentage of new conversions because, as we later came to understand, this phenomenon is broader than mere change of belief. But we note that, among those respondents whom we questioned, some 2-3 per cent were new conversions. Again we must reiterate that this was a sociological investigation of 'traditional' believers. So we can imagine that the phenomenon of conversion is spreading.

That is why it has seemed very interesting and useful to study this subject. We have already stated that in society misunderstanding of converts dominates. The majority think that these people are abnormal or paranormal; or that they are looking for privileges such as contacts with foreign religious communities, money or popularity. Of course, all these motivations exist, and we see that for some people religious activity is one of the new ways to achieve satisfaction of social ambitions, monetary gain or other advantages. But they are not the majority and concentrating on them will not help us understand the spread of this unusual phenomenon.

When we began to study the issue of new conversion we found in our nearest environment more than fifty families who had converted, and we started our investigation with them. That we are dealing with families is not accidental. When women or men change their faith, as a rule, this exerts a large influence on the whole family. As we will see later, inter-confessional or inter-ethnic marriages also tend to be accompanied by the conversion of the spouse.

During recent years (from 1986–93) we have carried out sociological surveys in schools and universities in the Republic of Tatarstan. Our results show us that the phenomenon of new conversion has become wide spread among youth. For example, in the years of state atheism there was serious commotion in high schools, when students in any way displayed their religious belonging. When one student in the Kazan Chemical Technological Institute was baptised, a Komsomol meeting was called and she was expelled first from the Komsomol and then from the Institute. Then the Kazan Conservatory discovered that several students were singing in church choirs, which caused a major crisis in the institution resulting in various administrative measures being applied to the students. When a case involved not the traditional and tolerated religions but non-traditional religiosity, this was equated with political unreliability. We can quote as an example the trial of the Krishna community in Moscow in the middle of the 1980s, or the example of a Krishna student, who was studying at the Technical Institute in Kazan at the beginning of the 1990s. Of course, the situation had by then completely changed and nobody openly persecuted him because of his religious belonging, but the attitudes of students compelled him to leave the Institute.

The situation has changed rapidly in the last two to three years. We can give one eloquent example. In one class of a Kazan school we discovered three pupils aged 15-16 years, belonging to three different denominations: Bahaism, Taoism (though we had never previously heard of adherents of this religion in Tatarstan and Russia), and Old Rite. All three came from areligious families. The other pupils in their class identified themselves with traditional, national religion. Practically none of them asserted atheism although, in fact, the majority were distanced from active adherence. Meanwhile, the pupil converts were very active not only in demonstrating their views but also in religious practice. It was remarkable that the attitude to them was far from one of condemnation of any 'abnormality'. Their religiosity, in their own views, was a symbol of their intellect, their superiority and exceptional character. We ought to mention that this was not an ordinary school, but special human sciences college. Of course, the situation in average schools will differ, but they also are very different from schools in previous years. These rapid changes in toleration of world-views and attitudes to religion are genuine in the younger generations, but for older people who have been brought up in the atmosphere of atheistic intolerance of religion the phenomenon of new conversion appears like something unusual.

Among converts we can distinguish two categories. The first are 'genetic believers': those who have converted to a religion traditional to their family or nation, but have done so at a mature age. We have stated earlier that among new converts we distinguish those whose religiosity is inherited, which is why we do not use the term proselytism in the sense of changing from one faith to another. We are studying 'genetic believers' in this context because the conversion has a common mechanism. Of course, 'genetic believers' do not arouse as much emotional reaction as other non-traditional converts, but even they encounter misunderstanding. Another definition of this phenomenon could be 'national believers' or 'national religiosity', as in the case of those Tatars who have been atheists in their youth and who adopt Islam in their old age.

The second are those who have converted to a religion which is traditional to the state or territory where they live, for example Tatars converting to Christianity, or Russians to Islam. This can be explained by the fact that the two cultures and religions have over the centuries lived and interacted with each other. An interesting example of the phenomenon of religious interaction occurs when Tatars celebrate Russian-Orthodox festivals and Russians vice versa (especially when Christmas and Kurban–Bairam were declared official holidays).

In this context we have to note the case of Tatar Christians (Kriashens) whose ancestors were converted to Orthodoxy in the 16th century after the conquest of Kazan by Ivan the Terrible or, as they themselves calculate, earlier. During these centuries some of them returned to Islam, but others have kept Christianity as their authentic religion.

After the collapse of the USSR, when the process of disintegration of the totalitarian state began, a national renaissance of Tatars as of all other peoples of the Soviet Union started. The idea that Islam is the foundation of the Tatar nation, the symbol of its identity, became very popular in the national movement. Of course, it caused some contradictions between Tatar Muslims, or those who used Islamic slogans in political movements or programmes, and the Kriashen who opposed the privileged position of Islam in sovereign Tatarstan. In the most popular and authoritative national organisation of Tatars, the Tatar Public Centre which asserted the special role of Islam in the history and culture of Tatars, a special section for Kriashens was organised. It now seems to be the case that Kriashens are developing as a sub-confessional group among Tatars.

It would appear that those who forecast a constant and endless process of disintegration of the totalitarian state were to a large extent right. The Soviet empire was a multinational state, and it collapsed. Russia and all the other Muslim republics of the former USSR are multinational and multi-confessional societies which is why the process of national and religious disintegration and political self-determination can have no end. But we see that there is another process parallel to decay, the process of integration. The CIS at first seemed to be an artificial and lifeless construction but we can see now that its components, and even those who have left, are trying to restore various forms of interaction.

In the case of Tatarstan there are also changes. Tatarstan was the first of the Russian autonomous republics which refused to sign the federal treaty. But Tatarstan was not as consistent as, for example, Chechnya, or maybe not as radical, and Chechnya for a time achieved much more independence than did Tatarstan. In February 1994 the treaty between Russia and Tatarstan was finally signed, and Tatarstan remained in the Russian Federation. For the adherents of the idea of sovereignty it seemed like a defeat in the political struggle, but the leaders of the republic explained the signing as a mutual compromise. In any case the integrative tendency dominated at this stage. As for the religious factor, it had little visible influence on the relationships between Russia and Tatarstan. In Chechnya, on the other hand, as M. Broxup wrote in the book *The North Caucasus Barrier* (p. 3), Sufi orders' support for Dudaev played a major role in the initially successful independence and break with Russia.

As we have already suggested, the important group of new converts are those whose conversion was the result of inter-ethnic or inter-confessional marriage. The focus of our interest was in the case of Muslim-Christian, Tatar-Russian families, and we discovered that the 'religious question' is real for the majority of them.

The problem of Muslim-Christian marriages has been discussed by a German observer M. Ahmed. He took the example of converts to Islam in Western Europe. He was told that among European converts a large proportion were converted by their husband or wife, usually the husband. But, he suggests, this conversion does not mean 'true religiosity'; and when these couples divorce, as very often happens, it causes a lot of conflict between Muslim and civil law expectations.

In Tatarstan the percentage of inter-ethnic marriages is very high:

in several towns (like Naberezhnye Chelny) every third family is mixed. Among them the majority are Tatar-Russian families. During our research we interviewed these families, and we have seen that there were several examples of conversion, but mainly to Christianity. There were only single cases of conversion to Islam. It is important to note that Islam does not prohibit inter-ethnic or inter-confessional marriages. According to the Sharia, a Muslim man may marry a non-Muslim women, but the reverse relationship is prohibited.

In Tatarstan, as we have said, there are many examples of the conversion of husbands to Christianity by Russian wives. Initially we were surprised by this fact, but after analysis of the situation in different multinational states and regions it became clear that this is common, especially for diasporas or national minorities in otherwise homogeneous societies. For example, I. Borowic has pointed out this situation in Poland concerning Tatars.

In our case the situation is practically the same. Tatars, even living in their own republic feel themselves as a minority in Russia. Even in the years of state atheism, official ideology opposed to religion and nationalism, was mainly based on the Russian culture and Orthodox values. Now there is a tendency to make Orthodoxy state religion, and in these circumstances the phenomenon of christianisation can be explained. The second explanation can be found in the linguistic sphere: we are told that for many Tatars the knowledge of their mother tongue is weak, so for these people Russian Christianity is closer than Tatar Islam. We must add that the situation in Tatarstan is such that the overwhelming majority of the Russian population does not know the Tatar language, despite the law about two state languages. For them, Islam is associated with Tatar religion and Tatar language.

During our researches we have met only one couple, a Russian family, converted to Islam. But we met about ten Tatar families, not of Kriashen origin, converted to Orthodoxy. It should be noted that the Muslim clergy totally neglects its Islamic missionary duty to propagate Islam to the different nationalities living not only in Tatarstan but also in Russia. All the sermons are in the Arabic and Tatar languages. Meanwhile the Orthodox clergy is more active in this field: for example, in one of the churches in Kazan the sermons are given in the Tatar language. This is explained primarily by the needs of the Kriashens, but we think that it exerts a significant influence on other parts of the Tatar population.

The problem of the status of religion in inter-confessional or inter-ethnic marriages in Tatarstan has many aspects. For example, when we surveyed school children in Kazan we discovered an interesting fact. The majority of them, Russians and Tatars, considered Islam to be the Tatar religion. They were absolutely sure that Islam prohibits inter-ethnic marriages (near 90 per cent of respondents of both groups). But more than 60 per cent of Tatar school children and nearly 80 per cent of Russians made the point that for them national and religious belonging does not play a role in the choice of future husband or wife.

Western researchers have pointed out that Tatars are one of the most assimilated nations in the ex-USSR, and we see that it is true to some extent, perhaps to a large extent. The example of language use and attitudes to inter-ethnic marriages among Tatars are eloquent indicators. Such assimilation is one of the reasons for the modern christianisation of Tatars.

The eleven families of new converts were those who changed their belief to different trends of Protestantism, non-traditional to the territory of Tatarstan. Among them were Tatars, Russians, mixed families and representatives of other nationalities.

We have said already that among denominations in Tatarstan there are several traditional ones. Before perestroika there were three Protestant denominations, but by 1993 the Council of Religious Affairs had registered nine Protestant denominations. Some of them, as for example Lutheranism, are based in the small part of the population of Kazan which is of German origin. But the others have been imported from different parts of the world, for example from Ukraine, from Germany or USA.

So, the third group are those who have adopted a religion not traditional to the region or are involved in 'new religious movements'. This category of new converts causes a lot of different emotional reactions and very often excite curiosity or suspicion in public opinion.

The working hypothesis of our investigation was the idea that the new converts, especially of this third group, are more 'religious', more active and more enthusiastic than traditional believers. It was very difficult to see how we could fulfil this task, because we discovered that we needed completely new criteria and typologies of consciousness and religiosity not available in Soviet-Russian philosophy and sociology of religion. Discussions in recent international conferences showed us that Western scholars also are not unanimous on this topic. For example, J. Waardenburg has said that the sociology of Islam has not yet been born in Western science. That can equally be said of modern Russian religious studies. In Western religious studies there is not, we have been led to understand, a generally accepted conception of 'true religion', 'implicit' or 'explicit' religion, etc.

In Soviet sociology of the past a theory of typology, indicators and criteria of religiosity was developed (general: Yablokov, with reference to Islam: Baltanov). In this sociology there were three types of religious consciousness: 'convinced believers', 'believers' and 'sympathisers'. If we extend this theory to the modern situation, we see that in fact there are no changes in the religious situation in Russia and Tatarstan. The level of actual religiosity ('convinced' believers), which means in reference to Islam fulfilling all the duties including propagation of the religion, is practically the same as in the years of 'state atheism'. Some of the current changes, such as religious revivalism, need a new theory of sociology of religion.

This is especially important when we are speaking about new religions or new converts. For example, speaking about Muslims one observes that the majority of those who identify themselves as Muslims do not practice regularly or at all. But is it correct to exclude them from the group of true believers and, on that ground, from our investigation? And how can we say that they are less religious than those who practise every day?

We have already mentioned that new converts are more active and more radical than typical believers. They fulfil all the demands of their religion and they are very active in propagating their faith. Many of them resign from their work (ten examples in our investigation) or they lose interest in the various forms of civil activity. For example Tatar converts are leaders of the Bahai community and Jehovah's Witnesses in Kazan; another Tatar man was the organiser and leader of the Evangelical community in Kazan, which is especially targeting Tatars. One Russian man is one of the activists of the recently organised (1992) Spiritual Board of Muslim Affairs of the Republic of Tatarstan after the former board split.

We have mentioned already that the third group of new converts attracts a lot of attention and is often the most disliked. Our research shows that the social basis of new religious movements is middle class, especially the intelligentsia. The median age is 30–35 years. Among them there are many students. This is also the typical picture of new religious movements in western countries.

It is very interesting to consider the lack of converts to Islam from people of non-Muslim nationalities. In the West this phenomenon is reportedly wide spread, and European Muslims often form special groups in the structure of believers. At the same time conversion to Islam is very slow even among customary Muslims. We have had many interviews with Tatar people brought up in sincerely Muslim families, but declaring themselves as non-believers.

Older people explain their non-belief with similar arguments. They often say, 'we are the lost generation', 'we were poisoned by propaganda', 'we were brought up as atheists' etc. When they were young they participated in religious rituals, but they do not remember the order of Muslim practice and think that it is very difficult to learn now. As for the young generation of Tatars, strongly Russianised and now living under the mass pressure of 'westernisation', for them Islam seems to be very strict with a wide system of different prohibitions.

Professor S. Shukurov believes that the weakness of conversion to Islam in the CIS, in comparison with the West, can be explained by the total destruction of the intellect, mentality and psychology during the period of colonisation and state atheism. In an article published in the newspaper of Russian intellectuals *Literaturnaya Gazeta* he wrote that ordinary post-Soviet Muslims, mainly determined by their custom, cannot grasp the ideas of the cultural and spiritual inheritance of their predecessors, cannot understand the poetry, philosophical tracts, or moral essays of Muslim writers and theologians. From his point of view these are losses which can be made good, and we agree with him.

During the period of state atheism religiosity was kept to its ritual, 'domestic' form, on the level of everyday religiosity. As several western Orientalists and Muslim scientists have said, Islam in the former USSR was preserved in the most conservative form. Modern Tatar historians and philosophers point out that the progressive traditions of Jadidism and the Tatar Enlightenment were lost. Perhaps this is one of the reasons why among new converts in Tatarstan there are few non-Tatar Muslims.

But despite all this we can not deny the growth of Islam among Tatars. The number of registered Muslim communities in the Republic of Tatarstan (333 out of the 444 communities registered) of course indicates the increasing number of Muslims. The full madrasas and mosques and the opening of the Islamic Institute in Kazan show us that despite the centuries of anti-Islamic policy in the Russian and Soviet empires, Islam survived and there is a process of Islamic renaissance in the Muslim republics of the CIS, very similar to the same process in all the Muslim world. This similarity can be explained by general, common features inherent in Islam. But this is a question for separate investigation.

Another group of new converts are those whom we can call, according to E. Barker's typology 'religiosity without belonging'. We think that they are the majority of the population of modern Tatarstan, as of modern Russia, according to the recent sociological researches of the Moscow Canter for the Study of Public Opinion. These are the people who agree with the questionnaire statement 'I believe in supernatural forces', identifying themselves confessionally. From a correct point of view they can be counted as believers or new converts, but they are really a reserve for conversion.

The following group of believers we can determine as the 'religious seekers'. They are searching for God or for gods and are even trying to create their own religious system. During our research we have met two examples of this phenomenon - two families who adopted Catholicism, then Orthodoxy and at this moment are in the stage of religious search.

Of course, the issue of conversion is particularly individual and very difficult to quantify. But when we began to study it we saw definite statistical regularities functioning, and we discerned several common factors determining the conversion. One of them is the 'border situation' described in existentialism. The majority of respondents told us that crisis, death, divorce, disease preceded their conversion. But this 'border situation' only disposes towards the adoption of religion.

So, a person has lost tranquillity and security, he is prepared for conversion, but there also must be an objective factor. Another cause is the missionary or 'propagandist' of faith. The fact that the missionaries of new religious movements or, for example, of neo-Protestantism are more active and experienced in their work in various alien environments can explain why they have more success than traditional denominations. We have mentioned already that the leaders of traditional confessions in Tatarstan are still very passive in search of modern, original forms of missionary activity. But there are exceptions: for example, the Muslim Board has restored the tradition of Qur'an reading competitions which gather people.

All the reasons we have mentioned are mainly of psychological character and they are of course very important for understanding the phenomenon of new conversion. But the social factors in the growth of this phenomenon is also a question of interest too. Soviet theory of the destiny of religion in socialist society was based on the Marxist theory of 'escaping' religion as socialism developed. And in the last years of Soviet socialism we saw that the process of secularisation was a constant and growing factor in spiritual life in the USSR. Even in Central Asia where the level of Muslim religiosity and ritual practice was very high (70–90 per cent depending on nation or region), one saw that Islam, which is not only religion (faith, cult, social institutions) but also *a modus vivendi*, lost the majority of its social functions. It did not fulfil economic, legislative and legal, integrative functions.

Of course, this observation cannot be extended to the Sufi orders in Central Asia or the Caucasian region, which survived because of the fact that Islam was the framework of this exclusive, to some extent esoteric, system. That is why there was a total misunderstanding of Sufism in all Soviet atheistic literature about Sufism in the USSR. In official propaganda it was often said that Sufism was a vestige or survival of the colonial past, when in fact Sufism was the basis of resistance to the colonial policy of the Russian Empire. We cannot ignore this reason, but the main factor in the survival of Sufism was that it was a specific socio-cultural system, capable of self-preservation. That could be true of Islam as a whole. But speaking about Tatarstan or the Muslim territories of Russia we see that secularisation was the reality precisely because Islam as a system was being destroyed.

We have mentioned already that the largest group of new converts are 'genetic' or 'national' Muslims. If we take the results of our investigations of 'traditional religions' in Tatarstan we see that there is a difference between Tatars and Russians in their attitude to 'their' religion. Practically 90 per cent of Tatars identified themselves as Muslims and the majority of them were new converts - those who some years before were non-believers.

It is important to note that the selections was done from those people whom we could classify loosely as believers, which is why the figure is so high. Of course, nobody would have guessed that the level of religiosity could raise so fast, especially as in the case of Islam we need the special system of up-bringing and education and the particular social conditions, for example, for the regular *salah*, for the fasting in the month of Ramadan, or for Hajj.

This large number of Muslims can be explained by those social factors we have begun to mention. Firstly, Islam is trying to restore social functions which had been lost: economic (the creation of Islamic banks, participation of Muslim Boards in economic activity), educational, political, the development of charity etc. This is the reason for the involvement of large numbers of people, even non-believers, in the confessional life.

Secondly, there is an ideological crisis in post-totalitarian society, and this ideological vacuum must be filled by a unifying and, most importantly, by a creditable system. We think that, as in the Muslim world generally, the ideology of nationalism is discredited to some extent by the failure of national organisations and movements in the political struggle, because of inter-ethnic conflicts or civil wars, because of the large number of mixed marriages and because of 'Sovietisation' which could not pass without leaving a trace.

An increasing role for religion in post-communist society is a general trend. It concerns not only Islam but practically all denominations in Tatarstan and Russia. So, the lack of the authoritative ideology is one of the factors in people turning to religion and conversion.

In conclusion, we want to say that the issue of new converts must be the subject of a special, wide investigation. The west which encountered new religious movements earlier than Russia and Tatarstan has extensive experience in studying the issue and in cooperating with these movements. In Tatarstan we still underestimate the scale of religious movements and conversion and tend to ignore them. Of course, we have moved far from atheistic methods of prohibiting non-traditional religious movements or condemning them. But we need to pay attention to the fact that these movements and conversions can cause different types of conflict. We know of many examples when child converts have left their families after quarrels with their parents. We know of families which have broken up.

The investigation of new religious movements in the former USSR has not yet begun. That is why we think it can be very useful to unite the efforts of Tatar and western scholars of religion in order to study this problem.

Notes

1. Baltanov, R., *Sotsiologicheskie problemy v sisteme nauchno-ateisticheskogo vospitaniya* (Sociological Problems in the System of Scientific and Atheistic Education). Kazan, 1973.
2. Avtorkhanov, A., et al., *The North Caucasus Barrier*, London, 1992.
3. *Vechernyaya Kazan*, 1991, 11, n. 4.
4. *Literaturnaya Gazeta*, 1991, 06, 05, N 22.
5. Yablokov I. *Religiya kak obshchestvennoe yavlenie. - Osnovy religiovedemiya. Lektsii k kursu.* (Religion as Social Phenomenon. In: Fundamentals of Religious Studies. Lectures for the Course. Novosibirsk, 1993.
6. Ahmed M. 'Muslim Women in Germany', *Journal of Institute of Muslim Minority Affairs*. Vol. 13, No. 2, 1992.

7

Ethno-Religious Minorities and Islamic Thought: the Volga Region and the Northern Caucasus

V. M. Viktorin

It is not infrequent that Christian-Muslim interaction takes place on the sub-ethnic level, for historically there have developed situations in which one part of a people adheres to Christianity and the other to Islam. These religious divisions within the same ethnic group (sub-ethnic entities), conscious of being one community, can be equal in size or one part of the sub-ethnic group may be much larger than the other. Although living together on a common site, they can either keep isolated from each other or be interspersed.

During periods of the community's ethno-political consolidation, the attitude to a minority of a different religious belief, and also the very status of the minority, often poses a problem which is not easily solved (especially at the level of public leadership and the intelligentsia).

It has always been difficult for dogmatic Islam to shape and define situations of this kind in terms of its categories, since the notion of 'umma' embraces at one time the 'commune' and the 'community', thus making it imperative to look at Muslims as one people (a 'nation' according to modern terminology), whereas Christians, Jews, and Zoroastrians are to be considered as representing other ethno-religious groups though depending on Islam. In the historical perspective, Islam happened to relate to several large ethno-linguistic entities: based on Arabo–Semitic foundations, it spread among Iranian and Turkic peoples. However, neither of these ethnic groups have become mono-religious despite powerful and impressive Islamisation. Different conditions and socio-political interests therefore stipulate a variety of approaches to a Muslim minority in a Christian ethnic environment and a Christian minority in a Muslim milieu. Of particular interest is the case of Tatarstan in Russia. There, an Islamised community (in which the non-believers and even the atheistic sections of the population are affected by Muslim traditions) lives in a Christian environment, while a large enough 'baptised' sub-ethnic group remains amidst a Tatar ethno-linguistic homogeneous totality. In a similar position in Russia today are also the Kabardinians of the Northern Caucasus. The growth of an 'all-Adyg' ethno-linguistic consciousness and a 'highlanders' territorial and political consciousness have generally intensified the formerly sporadic links of the main body of Muslim Kabardinians with a small but compact group of Christians of the so-called 'Malaya' ('small') or Mozdok Kabarda in Ossetia (as well as with the overseas diaspora of the latter group, the Austrian diaspora included).

As to the Persian speaking Ossetians themselves, the Muslim group among them, on the contrary, is an influential ethno-religious minority (as with the Abkhazians - the Adygs of Transcaucasia). At the same time, among the Persian speaking Tats in Dagestan and neighbouring Azerbaidjan there are, alongside a Jewish group ('highland Jews'), a Christian Armenian minority of Gregorian denomination (the 'Armeno–Tats') and two Muslim sub-religious minorities of Sunnis and Shi'ites.

But while in the Arab countries the attitude to the 'native' Arab Christians has long preoccupied the public mind, in Russia this kind of 'sub-ethno-religious' political science is just emerging, although the necessary conditions for its development began to take root in the past. This issue is unevenly tackled in the social science literature.

Among the scholars of Russia and the former Soviet Union who have devoted their research to the Arab–Muslim world the topics adopted which from our point of view are notable include the position and role of Christian groups in the Arab–Muslim world (A. N. Zhuravskii) and the prevailing theoretical approaches to the correlation between religion, nationality and ethnicity (R. Ya. Aliev).

The interpretation of the theoretical concepts of the classical East in the works of Volga Muslim thinkers has recently been tackled by R. M. Amirkhanov and A. N. Yuzeev. In previous decades, the development of socio-political thought in this region was considered by Ya. I. Nafiganov, K. F. Faseev, S. M. Mihailova, Ya. G. Abdullin,

Ya. I. Hanbikov amongst others. K. D. Davletshina, N. A. Ashirova, G. R. Baltanova and others have concentrated on national-religious topics. M. S. Totoev, Z. p. Tshovrebov focused on religious ethnic situations (Islam and Christianity in a traditional environment and the interpretation of their role) as well as ethno-religious situations (varied religious orientations in an ethnic group) in the Northern Caucasus and Ossetia.

Of major significance for the issues under consideration in this essay are the ideas of Arab–Christian theorists and publicists at the turn of the century (such as N. Azuri and F. Antun) about 'the single Arab nation' (*al-umma al-arabiyya*), which have been studied by some of the authors mentioned. Similar statements regarding ethnic unity can be found in the works of intellectuals representing the educational wing among the scholars of Turkic and Iranian origin in Russia such as Tatars Sh. Marjani, K. Nasyri and others, as well as A.-B. Tsalikov, an Ossetian by birth.

Claims made for the concept of 'nativism' (*pochvennichestvo* in Russian) are attractive for their tendency to be humane. But from the point of view of the terminology adopted in Soviet, and later on Russian, social science, the statement about 'nationalism as a unifying creed, religion' advanced in the 1940s jointly by a number of Arab Muslim and Christian theorists and politicians (M. Aflaq, A. Hourani, Y. Khalil and others) is open to debate. On the contrary, Orientalists from this country (I. M. Reisner, L. R. Gordon-Polonskaya, A. I. Ionova) consider the notion of Muslim nationalism as a destructive force which divides ethnic groups on the basis of religious affiliation

The main traditions of Arab–Muslim philosophy and political thought have not made a great impact on Muslim communities in Russia. In the absence in modern times of an Islamic state, and in an environment in which Muslims are invariably a minority, ideological trends rooted in the classical tradition have not developed at all or have found other forms of expression.

The Muslim tradition as a whole provides for a wide variety of approaches and attitudes to fellow countrymen of a different religious denomination, ranging from ignoring the very fact of their existence, through recognising the fact as such but with a serene neutrality, to a desire to unite (on grounds of the ethnic or religious affiliation of the majority), or to a categorical and decisive rejection. This diversity can be classified into three major types of approach to sub-ethno-religious minority groups: the traditionalist, modernist (progressivist) and radical fundamentalist models. They are reflected in public opinion, in the press, in the programmes and documents of parties and movements, and in the declarations of political leaders.

Traditionalism as a worldly mental disposition to which a majority of Muslims adhere generally considers co-existence with Christians (both inside and outside of ethnic community) as quite acceptable and natural. But as a politicised religious *Jadid* (reformist) movement, fundamentalism in Islam, while striving to restore the 'point of departure', artificially animated and constructed anew, generally refuses to acknowledge the right of Christians who speak the same language to exist and strives to convert them to Islam. Otherwise, 'according to the Qur'an' they are doomed to play a subordinate and dependent role, with restrictions imposed, some of a humiliating nature. 'Up till now, fundamentalists consider even Arab Christians to be dhimmis.'[1]

Modernism advocates a wide variety of innovations, from an orientation toward 'modern' Islam to slogans proclaiming a secular state, secularised civil society, freedom of worship and equality of faith (within 'one's own' ethnic community, among others). This approach advocates borrowing from other cultures including Western culture.[2]

In Muslim socio-political (and pedagogical) thought in the Middle Volga region at the turn of the 20th century, fundamentalist tendencies were represented by the so-called *qadimiyya* trend ('antique' in Arabic). Its followers (mullahs I. Dinmuhamedov, I. Muhutdinov, Sh. Muhammadiyev, S. Ishakov and others) converted Islam into a dogma repudiating everything related to the *kafir*s as intolerable.

An opposite trend identified as Jadidism, underwent a complicated evolution personified by its spokesman (G. Utyz-Imyani, Sh. Marjani, K. Nasyri, Sh. Kultyasi, M. Miyazova, H. Fazhanova, the Halfin brothers and others) from moderate modernisation based on Islam (Islamic reformism) to a demand to combine the spiritual with the secular both in education and social life (cultural and educational activities).[3] Teaching secular subjects at school and an emphasis on the role of the Russian language were characteristic of the activities of the educators of the Jadid movement.

The thinker Husain Faizhanov, while responding to the *qadimiyya* teacher Ismagil Kyshghari, who claimed that learning 'the language of the kafirs' was a sin, made very important comments regarding religion and ethnicity. According to him, the Russian language

... is also used by the inhabitants of the Sloboda [a section of urban Tatars], and these have been Muslims for a long time. Or take the Persian language: it is spoken by Muslims, by many pagans from non-Arab countries, and by the Jews. Now, some Tatars in eastern countries who are idol worshippers speak our language ... There is one thing you should understand: in the majority of cases the language happens to be common both for Muslims and the *kafirs*.[4]

The 'sub-ethnoreligious' issue involving Tatar Christians – the 'Starokriashens' who adopted Christianity in the 16th century, and the 'Novokriashens' who were converted from Islam at some time in the 18th century – did not as such truly preoccupy the reformers. For historians, they were just a small and insignificant Tatar community that isolated itself (according to them under conditions hardly favourable during the conquest). On the other hand, for politicians both before and after the revolution the intelligentsia of the Kriashens were potentially a force in favour of baptism and Russification. After the revolution these converts, together with other 'Christian' peoples of the Volga region, had to be taken into account in the process of state building. The famous Sultan-Galiev referred to the Kriashens with just these two aspects in mind.[5]

The fact is that the educational process among the Kriashens was of a specific 'non-Muslim' type, although their role in the education of other Volga Christians and in the development of methods applied in the process was significant.

At present, the issue of the Kriashen Tatars is again in the public eye. This is due to the general upheaval of popular movements, the Tatar movement as a whole and that of the Kriashens in particular. It is also an effect of the political consciousness becoming 'historical', while the not yet fully investigated events of 1552 relating to the conquest of the Kazan Khanate give an additional flavour and impulse to political slogans and actions. The open minded clergy of the Muslim Religious Board (Talgat Tazhutdin, etc.), who hold to the traditional approach to Islam, display complacency as well as a degree of confidence and moderation in the way they behave.

The change of outlook of the Tatar Public Centre (TPC) as well as of the Milli Majlis (the alternative parliament of the Tatar people) has not been accidental as far as the Kriashen Tatars are concerned. Organised in December 1990 as a section of the first Ethnographic Cultural and Educational Association of Kriashens, it seceded from it as early as July 1992 and joined, as an independent organisation, the Association of National Cultural Societies of the Republic of Tataristan, while the Committee of Baptised (Kriashen) Tatars, founded in August 1992, never started its work.

The above facts have immediate relevance to the radicalisation of the activities of both politicised public bodies and to their growing 'Muslim' component. The attitude of the Tatar National Independence Party, Ittifaq, and of the youth movement Azatlyk was from the very start negative towards the Christian Orthodox Tatars. A negative attitude would be displayed by the *Iman* newspaper: the Kriashens were 'a second time offered to adopt Islam'.

The position of Moscow Muslim circles proved to be the same. Ravil Gainutdin, the *imam-hatib* of the Moscow Jamia Mosque and president of the Moscow Islamic Centre, repeatedly made pronouncements in favour of Islam as the only ideological guard of the Tatar nation, and reiterated the statement about 'forcible baptism' of the Kriashens and the danger they present of 'levelling' the Tatars.[6] Similarly, the fundamentalist-oriented political organisation, Nahdat, founded in Astrakhan on 9 June 1990,[7] does not accept Christianity among the Tatar people, judging by the declarations of its leaders. The modernist/progressivist approach to the ethnic and religious minorities in Tataristan is primarily represented by the republic's leadership which adopts a moderate approach to the issue.

On the other hand, the Kriashens themselves have joined ranks. The Kriashen paper, prohibited since the 1920s, resumed publication in February 1993. Now it is put out in Naberezhnye Chelny under the title of *Kriashen Suze* ('The World of the Kriashen'). Although not a single church has remained intact in areas inhabited by the Kriashens, some parishes have in recent years started a new liturgy in the Tatar language. The activists of the Kriashen national movement for the revival of culture as well as professional historians are producing some interesting publications that question the claim that Kriashen Tatars were forcibly baptised as well as the connection between these developments and the conquest of 1552.[7]

Different tendencies obtain in the Tatar communities of Russia outside Tataristan. In Bashkortostan, one can observe the Muslim and Kriashen Tatar population unite on the basis of a common culture. In the Cheliabinsk region, however, a group of Kriashen re-settlers from Tataristan, irregular warriors (the so-called *nagabaiks*) seem to have begun developing, following the 'Lebano–Syrian' model, a specific religious though Tatar-speaking nationality.[8]

In the Astrakhan district, among Tatar re-settlers from the Middle Volga region, are some families who come from the *novokriashens*, i.e. those who were converted to Christianity from Islam as early as the 18th century and became Muslims again in the early 20th century. They differ only by their surnames of 'Russian' type (the Pozdniakovs, the Yevseevs, the Nikitins, the Vassilievs, etc.) combined with Muslim first names. And only very few people are knowledgeable enough to identify their specific origin.

Members of the Tatar youth club 'Umet' who keep constantly in touch with the Kazan 'Azatlyk' are notable for their intolerant attitude to the sign of the cross (the representation has been retained by the former Christian refugees who find themselves today in the areas of regional Tatar society). As to the Kriashens, they categorically declare, 'These people are not ours!' However, the traditional conservatism of local Islam, of the older generation of believers as well as of the major part of the 'educated', official priesthood, has prevented the activities of the fundamentalist reformist group of the Islamic Revival Party from taking root in Astrakhan.

The Kriashen village of Bolshoi Shurniak (Elabuga district in Tataristan) surrounded by Muslim–Tatar, Russian and Mari villages, visited by the author in August 1993, is an example of loyalty and tolerance both of Islamic and Christian traditionalism.[9] Together with the neighbouring Muslim Tatar village, Bolshoi Shurniak has until recently formed a common collective farm. According to local popular belief among the Kriashens, during a dry season one ought to invite Muslim neighbours for a public prayer in the old cemetery located behind the village. Behind visible Christianity an ancient shamanistic ('pagan') cultural layer is discernable: while at one end of the village at the crossroads a small chapel has been restored, on the other end, on the former edge of the forest there is still an old dried up pine tree to which sacrifices were made in past decades. Thus, traditionalism on both sides is connected with multiple religious sub-ethnic syncretism.

Highland peoples of the Caucasus that include groups of Muslims and Christians are, incidentally, well aware of this kind of syncretism (based on shamanism) which is an important unifying factor and includes worship at the same holy places which reflect both the pre-Christian and pre-Islamic past.

However, it is not on the everyday level, but on the ideological and theoretical one, that the civilisational orientations of people belonging to different religions within one ethnic group can be altogether different. It is the new consolidation, this time ideologically based, that is often preceded by a tendency towards separation. Thus, within Ossetian culture, literature and socio-political thought, Christian Orthodox (K. Hetagurov) as well as Islamic (A.-B. Tsalikov, B. Turanov) trends show up.

Both the Christian–Kriashen group among the Tatars of Tataristan and the Muslim–Ossetian group on the territory of Northern Ossetia constitute notable and influential 'ethno-religious minorities'; it is only due to the fact that the Ossetians are in general less numerous than the Tatars that their Islamic branch gives an illusionary impression of being significant.

If the Kriashens make up less than 5 per cent of the Tatars living in a solid community in the Middle Volga region (they are over 100,000 out of 1,750,000 Tatars in the Republic of Tataristan), the number of Muslims among the sub-ethnic group of Digora Ossetians (who account for one eighth of the Ossetians of Northern Ossetia) amount to (as indicated by different sources) 30–40 per cent, and to 20–30 per cent among the predominant Iron Ossetians.

Incidently, this recalls another not less erroneous impression popular in Western writings about the exceptionally 'Muslim character' of the Digora Ossetians. The prevalence of traditional Muslims in Ossetia is ensured by the Iron Ossetian group (in the east and south-east of the republic).[10]

While, as recorded during pre-revolutionary times, up to one third of the Ossetians observed Muslim traditions in everyday life, at present it is possible to roughly identify among the overall Ossetian population of Northern Ossetia up to 5 per cent of observant Digora people and up to 20 per cent of Iron people (out of 335, 000 Ossetians living in the republic).

Islam is believed to have found its ways to Ossetia as early as the 9th–10th centuries. and later on during the Mongol–Tatar presence, but made its most energetic advance through Kabarda (bordering on Digora) in the 17th–18th centuries. Hence, the prominence of Islamic tendencies in the culture, ideology and politics of the Ossetians in their historical tradition, such as 'kabardinism' (the Ossetian *kasaggade*).[11]

The major tendencies in Muslim socio-political thought (including the attitudes of Ossetian Christians), both in ideology and everyday life, manifest themselves in rather peculiar forms, the 'Northern Caucasus' variant also being taken into account. They are not as explicitly expressed as in the Middle Volga region (the less so if compared with the Near East and the Arab, Muslim countries in general). It is also necessary to take into account the powerful polytheistic ('paganistic') shamanistic elements, very real and well understood by most Ossetians (as distinct from the situation typical of the Tatars in the Middle Volga region). But this element is reflected and assessed differently by the people and the clergy of different religions, even the priests from individual sub-ethnic groups.

One can talk about 'multiple' traditionalism in the Ossetian environment, ethno-cultural traditionalism only marginally oriented towards religious beliefs. Generally speaking, traditional Muslims can have Christian rather than Muslim names (the president of Northern Ossetia, Professor Ahsharbek, a philologist, the son of Hajmurza Galazov, despite his Muslim-sounding name, descends from a long Christian lineage). One can talk about traditionalism based on a religious (polytheistic–shamanistic) substratum uniting all the Ossetians in general. And, finally, one can also speak of traditionalism in each of the two world religions prevailing in Ossetia, Islamic traditionalism in particular.

Concerning the problem of 'traditionalism', the Ossetian businessman and politician, Valeri, leader of the 'Eurasian Humanitarian' movement in the republic, remarked:

> As a result of mixing pre-Christian beliefs with Christianity and Islam, there appeared in Ossetia a specific creed which embraced all the faiths and ideas mentioned above. Consequently, and in many respects curious triple symbiosis of archaic, Christian and Islamic notions came into being.[12]

The effects of modernity will be felt in the future. Thoughtful experts point to a gradual but continuous growth of the impact of the Digora Ossetian sub-ethnic group on the state of affairs in the republic, and within it, the growth of influence of its Muslim Iraf subgroup thus called after the name of the administrative district where its members live. Even now, a very large section among the intelligentsia of Vladikavkaz, the capital of the republic, is represented by Iraf

Ossetian people. It is these people who make pronouncements in favour of the restoration of the Digora dialect of the Ossetian language (the most ancient in form but not corresponding to the standard contemporary Ossetian language). The paper *Digora* and, to a lesser extent, the magazine *Iraf* that are issued in Vladikavkaz can be considered the mouthpieces of the interests and views of this group.

Attempts to introduce elements of religious fundamentalism in the Ossetian environment were made from outside at the time of the Soviet collapse. These were connected with purely political attempts at uniting 'Muslim' peoples and groups along the southern perimeter of Russia, the impact of the Confederation of Highland Peoples of the Caucasus (formed on the basis of Kabarda Adygs), the developments in Chechnya (Ichkeria) and the territorial conflict between Ossetia and Ingushetia. However, traditionalist principles triumphed: political and ethnic interests must have influenced the process as well as the significant distinctions between different brands of Islam – those characteristic of the Ossetians (Alans) and the Vainakhs (Chechens and Ingushes, the former being Hanafis and the latter Shafi'is, with Sunnism as such being of general significance for both).

The ancient system of belief of the Ossetians is discernible in their world-view, customs and rituals, folklore, toasts and greetings. Its manifestations are somewhat different among Ossetian Christians (it almost fully embraces Christian dogmas and assimilates them) and Muslims in various regions. Muslims treat 'heathenism' in a more restraint manner, especially the Digora Ossetians, while the Iron Ossetians are often trying to find 'meeting points' in their everyday notions with the principles of Islam. Even the 'more devout' Digora Ossetians follow suite.

The traditional religion of the Ossetians is a transitory stage from polytheism to monotheism ('genotheism', 'ethnotheism') when out of a plurality of gods the only one, the major one is singled out. With the Ossetians such a major deity is Styr Hystau or Hstau (the literary pronunciation is the Iron Shtyr Hshtau) i.e. 'the Great Magnificent God', or Yunak Hstau, 'the Single God'. The leading figure of the Ossetian pantheon is Uastardzhy or Uashtardzhy (in Digora it is Uaskergi), the protector of men, warriors and travellers that has merged with the Christian image of St George.

In the Ossetian valleys, each locality inhabited by people has a sanctuary called *dzuars* or *dzhuars* (Georgian *dzhvari*, the cross) dedicated to Uastardzhi and other deities; they are often attended to by priests, or initiators, the *dzuarsags* (the Iron *dzhuarshags*) that remind one of the ministers of shamanism of the latest period. Here are held community festive prayers called *kuvd*s.

In the village of Elhotovo (of Iron Muslim origin), an ancient place famous for its archaeological value, the administrative centre of the Kirov district, both Muslim cult priests and ordinary believers are prone to think that 'Allah is Shtyr Hyshtau and Uashtardhzy is his prophet'. Behind the village is the Uashtardhzy *dzhuar* where each November a *dzhorgoba* (a community *kuvd* thus called after St George) is held. Formerly, not far off across the Terek, at the site of the medieval settlement of Tatartup, an annual 'jahiliyya in Islam' was held to worship the 'Tatartup deity' that was esteemed by many Ossetians.[13]

The continuing influence of 'heathenism' in the Digora Ossetian group of Muslims is well illustrated by the following. On a February morning in 1992, in the centre of the village of Chikola (Chikola being the administrative centre of the Iraf district), there were discovered imprints of huge wings, with the wing-span over one metre large, as well as hoofs in the snow on the roof of the house belonging to mullah Hasan Kardanova. This is considered by the Ossetians to be an indisputable sign of the place having been visited by Uaskergi (St George) himself. Then, with the support of the mosque and the official district authorities, a grand public holiday for all the village dwellers, the *kuvd*, was celebrated on the street of the Kardanovs' house, in commemoration of the miraculous event. The holiday took place again in February 1993 and in 1994.[14]

Despite the specific character of Ossetian Islam, one can detect the existence of both a more 'potent' Iraf Digora traditionalism that is closer to Muslim dogmas (at least in rhetorical terms) and a weaker Iron Ossetian traditionalism of an abstract nature (on the right bank, at the city of Beslan, Kirov District).

Returning to the subject of traditionalism (all-Ossetian, ethnic and, to some extent 'pagan'), it is also possible to suggest that it is just such traditionalism that the authorities of the republic are trying (and it looks as if they are likely to continue trying) to make use of, supported by the national public movements and their executive bodies, for the sake of consolidation and integration of the Ossetian people (of Southern and Northern Ossetia), in spite of the existence of sub-ethnic and even more fractional subdivisions and religious orientations.

This status of a common national symbol is ever more attributed to one of the main *dzuar*s, the so-called Hetaga sacred grove (*Hetaji juar* or *Jyng'ysh*) situated between Vladikavkaz and Alagir. Here, too, the public holiday – the Hetaga Day – is celebrated each year in July. In the spring and early summer of 1994, the All-Ossetian Council Styr Nyhas (more correctly, Shtyr Nyhash) that enjoys the full support of the president and the government was the most active in clearing the territory of the grove of irrelevant buildings and protecting beech and elm trees against gatherers of wood, casual visits and pollution. Once every fortnight, public *subbotnik*s (voluntary unpaid work on days off) took part in improving the condition of the holy place. A special Hetaga Grove Council was set up. Regulations concerning the sacred grove were under preparation.

The president of the Styr Nyhas board, M. I. Gioev stated 'we do not want to hurt anybody's religious feelings, neither Christian, Muslim, sectarian or any other ... While reinstalling sanctuaries, we proceed from the fact that Ossetian culture and way of life are, as it were, naturally connected with the *dzuar*s ... and we are to turn the *dzuar*s into true centres of moral, aesthetic education but not into places for enjoying drinks and food ... As never before, the *dzuar*s are badly needed during dramatic historical periods.'[15]

The legend of Hetag and his grove is almost forgotten nowadays and preserved only in scattered writings with immediate reference to the topic under consideration. Hetag, a Kabardinian nobleman and the son of the ranking prince Inal, was considered to be founder of the Hetagurovs' lineage and direct ancestor in the tenth generation of the pride of the Ossetians. The famous writer poet and educator Konstantin or 'Kosta', was the son of Levan Hetagurov (1859–1906). Having adopted Christianity being a Muslim and persecuted by his brothers, Hetag fled from Kabarda to Ossetia, and on his way he was unexpectedly hidden from his persecutors by a magic grove (until now called 'the Hetag Grove') that all of a sudden fell out of the sky.[16]

By the way, being descendent of an old Christian lineage, K. L. Hetagurov has carefully and vividly described the life of Muslims in his 'Caucasian tale of verses' entitled 'Fatima', thus contributing to the dissemination of this Muslim name (but with the stress on the second syllable) among contemporary Ossetian girls in Christian families.

Among the Ossetians, the 'Hetag Grove' is believed to be a most proper place for Wastarji worshipping. The cult of this saint calls for close attention and it is also inevitably used by Ossetian politicians. 'It is no secret that the unity and indivisibility of our nation is affected by religious disunion... A unique ideology that would be able to knit the nation together is wanted. In terms tending towards monotheism this would fit more the Wastarji cult.'[17]

In this case, one might with good reason talk about tendencies or even a process of 'reverse traditionalism', about the 'politicisation of paganism' that manifests itself in a different way in the Baltic republics and among particular socio-professional groups of the Russian people. Though yet hardly discernable in the traditional Muslim environment, it is progressing fast in the adjacent zone of the Middle Volga region, Chuvashia (Chavash En) and especially in Mariy El.[18]

Summing up, one should emphasise the need for the people of different religious beliefs, common origin, language and destiny (traditionalism) to be live peacefully together side by side with each other, and the desirability of them participating on an equal footing in the onward development of society, native cultures and countries (modernisation).

The unusual, sometimes paradoxical variety of human culture, ethnic and religious cultures included, is a reality of the modern world. And the future trends of its evolution, whether along the path of integration or differentiation, require close consideration in each particular case. Important individual examples of such processes and their reflection in diverse social and political ideas have been investigated in the present article.

In conclusion, I should like to cite a remarkable example of coincidence of a constructive attitude assumed by representatives of ethno-religious minorities aware of their role and specific character, who proceed from their culturally 'marginal' status and therefore comprehend their calling and considerable responsibility.

It was A. B. T. Tsalikov, a Muslim Ossetian, head of the executive committee of the All-Russian Muslim National Council in the beginning of 1917, who said:

> We are the vanguard of the Islamic world that has edged its way onto the European continent. We find ourselves between two cultures. That is why we, Muslims of Russia, have to fulfil our duty and carry the great ideas, the light of freedom we ourselves enjoy, to the whole of the East, to the Islamic world at large.'[19]

N. Edelbi, professor at a theological college in Jerusalem, wrote in the early 1950s:

We need Western culture ... to exercise our mediatory mission between the East and the West ... The Christians ought to be conscious of their social mission which will help them overcome their religious prejudices ... understand the legitimate aspirations of modern Islam and promote their realisation, while remaining Christians.[20]

Such a coincidence of views is indicative of a perceived common humanity. It implies common tasks and tendencies in the development of different religions in 'marginal' situations of cultural interaction. It also shows through what means it is possible to abstain from simpler aspirations – differences and enmities or estrangement and self-isolation.

Notes

1. Aliev R.Ya. 'Etnokonfessionalnye problemy:islam i panarabskie kontseptsii', *Etnokonfessionalnye protsessy v sovremennom mire* (Baku 1989), p.55 ('Ethnoreligious Problems: Islam and Pan-Arab Concepts', *Ethnoreligious Processes in the Contemporary World*).

2. See: Zhuravskii A.B. 'Hristianstvo i islam', *Sotsiokulturnye problemy dialoga* ('Christianity and Islam', Sociocultural Problems of Dialogue) (Moskva 1990), pp. 93–104.

3. See: Yuzeev A.N. *Mirovozzrenie Mardjani i arabo-musulmanskaya filosofia*, (Marjani's World Outlook and the Arab–Muslim Philosophy) (Kazan 1992).

4. Cited from: Abdullin Ya. G. *Tatarskaya prosvetitelskaya mysl* (Tatar Educational Thought) (Kazan, 1976), p. 237.

5. See: Mirsaid Sultan-Galiev. *Stati, vystuplenia, dokumenty*, (Articles. Speeches. Documents) (Kazan 1992), pp.35, 314, 409.

6. 'Kak stat musulmaninom?', Russkopalestinskaya gazeta *Al-Kods*, Moskva, ('How to become a Muslim?', Russian–Palestinian newspaper *Al-Kods*; 1993, mai, no. 6 (12), c.11 'Ne nado boyatsa istinnogo fundamentalizma', gazeta *Moskovskii komsomolets*, ('One needn't be afraid of true fundamentalism', newspaper *Moskovskii komsomolets*) 1993, 20 iyula, no. 136, s.2.

7. See for greater detail: Viktorin V.M. 'Natsionalnii faktor vo vzaimootnosheniah gosudarstva, tserkvi i obshchestvennyh organizatsii (po materialam Astrahanskoi oblasti)', *Gosudarstvenno–tserkovnye otnoshenia v Rossii*, ('The national factor in the relationship between the state, the church and social organizations (based on the materials of the Astrakhan area)', *Relations Between the State and Church in Russia*). (Moskva 1993), pp. 69–74.

8. See: Gluhov M.S. (Nogaibek). *Sudba gvardeitsev Seyumbeki. Neformalnyi podhod k yestcho nepisanym stranitsam istorii*, (The Destiny of the Seyumbeki Guardsmen. A Non-Formal Approach to the Not Yet Written Pages of History). Kazan 1993.

9. See: Hudoborodov A.L. *Nagaibaki (Iz istorii kazachestva Urala)*, (The Nagaibaks. From the History of the Urals Cossacks). Chelabinsk 1992.

10. Data from the field diary of the author.

11. See: Uarziati V.S. 'Islam v kulture Osetii', *Eho Kavkaza*, Zhurnal Assotsiatsii narodov Kavkaza ('Islam in the culture of Ossetia', *Echo of the Caucasus*, Journal of the Association of the Peoples of the Caucasus)(Moskva 1993), N.3, pp. 18–19.

12. See: Viktorin V.M. 'Musulmanstvo Osetii i Ingushetii (nasha spravka)', gazeta *Vestnik*, Organ vremennoi administratsii v raionah chrezvychainogo polozhenia ('Islam in Ossetia and Ingushetia (materials for information), *Vestnik*, newspaper of the provisional administration in emergency areas. (Vladikavkaz 1994), 14. aprelia, N.13 (86), p. 1.

13. Kairov V.M. *Traditsii i istoricheskii protsess* (Traditions and the Historical Process).
(Moskva 1994), pp. 128–9

14. Data from the field diary of the author.

15. Data from the field diary of the author.

16. 'Vtoroye rozhdenie rostchi Hetaga', gazeta *Severnaya Osetia*, ('The second birth of the Hetaga Grove', newspaper *Northern Ossetia*). (Vladikavkaz 1994), 2 aprelia, N.62, p.4

17. See: Hetagurov K. (L.) *Byt gornyh osetin (etnograficheskii ocherk)* (Mode of Life of Highland Ossetians (a study in social anthropology), (Staliniri 1939), pp.6-7.

18. Bidzhelov B.H. 'O nashem yedinstve', gazeta *Severnaya Osetia* ('About our unity', newspaper *Northern Ossetia*).(Vladikavkaz 1994), 23 marta, N.54, p. 2.

19. See: 'Sotaya yeparhia. Poslednii yazycheskii narod Evropy', *Nezavisimaya gazeta* ('The hundredth diocese', *Nezavisimaya gazeta*) (Moskva 1994), 17 marta, no. 50, p. 5.

20. Cited from: Ashirov N. *Islam i natsii* (Moskva 1975), p.87 (*Islam and Nations*); see also Tsalikov Ah. *Kavkaz i Povolzhye. Ocherki inorodcheskoi politiki i kulturno-hoziastvennogo byta*, (The Caucasus and the Volga Region. Essays on Non-Russian Politics, Cultural and Economic Life) Moskva 1913.

21. Cited from: Zhuravskii A. B. *op.cit.* p. 110.

8

Muslims in Moscow: An Ethnic and Social Portrait of the Interior of a Russian City

Aida Moseyko

Russian history testifies to long-standing contacts and interactions between Slav and Muslim (primarily Turkic) ethnic groups. In the geopolitical space of Russia there were not only the regions with mainly Muslim inhabitants (in the former Soviet Union and Autonomous Republics), but ethnically dispersed groups in the regions with Russian population particularly in large Russian towns. The status of these groups, migration processes within them, their ethnic, cultural and social orientations cannot be analysed in isolation from the general regional and historical problems of the main ethnic group of the territory and of other peoples, united by a common historical destiny. It is of particular importance since the civilisation of Russia represented a combination of Western and Oriental tendencies, not only Slavs but also the representatives of other peoples (including Muslims) who have played a role of no small importance in its formation.

The Turkic-Muslim influence on the Russian culture manifests itself, for example, in a number of words of Turkic origin in the Russian language (there are more than 500 of them); in the street names of the Russian towns (Arbat and Ordynka in Moscow); in the origin of Russian family names (Dashkovs, Aksakovs, Yusupovs, Saltykovs, Mamonovs, Kudashovs and others). The signs of this influence can be found in Russian folk-lore ('The Lay of Igor's Host', tales, folk-songs), in Russian literature (in Pushkin's writings for example). The influence of Russian culture on Muslim culture is undoubted.

Interactions of cultures are particularly noticeable in towns, where the Muslim migrants have a considerable influence on the urban culture and the mode of life, and where they in their turn are subjected to the influence of Russian culture. The large towns of Russia are multiethnic conglomerates, in which there is coexistence of groups with different historical past, different confessions, cultures, and mentalities. The most typical of the multiethnic and multiconfessional towns is Moscow, where the representatives of more than 100 nationalities live.

Among the groups of permanent non-Russian residents in Moscow Muslims are second in number, after the Ukrainians. They include representatives of many Muslim ethnic groups: Tatars, Azerbaidjanis, Uzbeks, Kazakhs, Ossetians, Bashkirs, Kirghiz, Tajiks, Chechens, Turkmens, and Daghestanis. Recently, in connection with the stream of migrants from 'the hot spots' (areas of intense ethnic conflicts) the number of such Muslim groups has abruptly increased.

Many of these Muslim groups live beyond their national states for both historical and political reasons. For example, the Tatars have historically been settled in different regions of present-day Russia (the Tatars of Siberia, Kazan, Astrakhan, Kasimov and so on).

Many peoples settled beyond their historical territories as a result of the forced deportations of Stalin's regime (the Ossetians, the Lezgins and the Chechens). By 1990 the following percentages lived outside their national states: Tatars 73.4; Kazakhs 19.7; Nogayans 62.4; Uzbeks 15.3; Lezgins 56.1; Azerbaidjanis 14.3; Ossetians 33.1; Kirghiz 11.8; Tajiks 24.7; Chechens 23.2; Turkmens 7.[1]

A large number of the representatives of Muslim groups, which are located out of their historical territories, have settled in large towns around Russia and above all in Moscow and St. Petersburg.

According to the results of the 1989 population census[2] 229,535 representatives of different Muslim groups lived in Moscow making up 2.6 per cent of the total population of the city (Russians 89.7 per cent). The largest Muslim groups of Moscow's permanent population are shown in Table 1. As one can see from the table, the Tatars are the largest group followed by Azerbaidjanis.

The Tatar population in Moscow increased through migration from the villages and other places of permanent residence, but the nucleus of this population are the descendants of those Tatars who settled in Moscow before the 19th century.

Table 1

Muslim Groups Resident in Moscow 1989

Ethnic group	Total	% of total population
Tatars	157,615	1.8
Azerbaidjanis	20,727	0.2
Uzbeks	9,183	0.1
Kazakhs	8,225	0.09
Ossetians	7,270	0.08
Bashkirs	5,417	0.06
Kirghiz	3,044	0.03
Tajiks	2,893	0.03
Chechens	2,101	0.02
Turkmens	2,093	0.02

The settlement of the Tatars in Zamoskvorechye (the Tatar sloboda) of Moscow is mentioned as early as the 17th century. By the end of the 17th century three groups of Tatars had formed in the city:

1. The representatives of the Tatar feudal nobility who were in the Tsar's service. Those with permanent residence in Moscow were: the tsarevitches (princelings) of Kasimov and Siberia (different Tartar ethnic groups), the Yusupov, Sheydyakov and Kutumov princes of the Nogay lineage, the Crimean Sulemov princes etc.
2. Owners of courtyards: translators and interpreters, traders, fortune-tellers, etc.
3. Dependent people who were in somebody's service, many of them descended from the captive Crimean and Nogay Tatars.

In the 18th century these three groups experienced considerable changes. The first – the Tatar nobility – underwent assimilation to a considerable extent. Its representatives adopted Christianity and joined the ranks of the Russian aristocracy, retaining only their family names – Yusupov, Kudashov, Kutumov and others. *Assimilés* of the Tatar nobility were motivated primarily by the interests of career and property. After the capital was transferred to St. Petersburg the aristocracy and a part of the second group moved there. The Tatar traders who traded with Siberia, Central Asia and Europe stayed in Moscow because of its geographical location. The third group also underwent considerable assimilation not only with Russians, but with Germans and the Poles of the German *sloboda*, where the Tatars were in service. The second group of the Tatars – traders, translators, interpreters – underwent least assimilation of all, living in a district where other ethnic Muslim groups had also settled.

At the end of the 19th century, fourteen large Tatar and some Azerbaidjani trading families lived in Moscow. In the traders' environment bilingualism was common, but national traditions were ardently maintained, educational work in the spirit of Islam was organised, and money for the traditional Muslim festivals was collected.

Moscow Tatar intellectuals knew Russian and Russian literature perfectly well but also remained true to their ethnic and confessional traditions and the Muslim culture. These traditions continue today and the majority of Tatar families honour national and Muslim customs, sometimes more ardently than people of Tatarstan and other Muslim regions.

The coexistence of different ethnic groups, particularly those representing different civilisations, depends to a large extent on the distribution of the social roles among them. In Moscow business and employment patterns were established amongst the Muslim population, elements of which are still in existence. These are peculiar ethnic and social niches, which from generation to generation were occupied by the representatives of certain Muslim groups. Among Moscow Tatars by the beginning of the 20th century, 38 per cent were occupied with commerce. They traded in cotton, silk, fur, leather and products of leather. The geographical situation of Moscow between Siberia, Central Asia and Europe created favourable conditions for commerce. Trade encouraged petty domestic industry, in which about 20 per cent of the Tatars were occupied: treatment and tincture of fur, furriery, dressmaking, sewing articles of fur and leather. Over 30 per cent worked in state institutions and served in the army; the representatives of clergy and intellectuals also should be included here. About 4 per cent of the Tatars owned doss-houses and eating-houses, or were in service, in particular as yard keepers, while over 5 per cent were draymen, railwaymen, carpenters, factory workers.

As the figures cited testify, almost 70 per cent of the Tatars were occupied in branches demanding some degree of literacy, in the main in the Russian language.

The employment structure of the Azerbaidjani population (considerably smaller than the Tatars both in numbers and in degree of stability) was formed on the basis of trade in oil and oil-products. Among the Azerbaidjanis in Moscow there were international oil merchants and also the owners of shops trading in kerosene. It is quite natural that about them groups of Azerbaidjanis developed including technical intellectuals and interpreters, who facilitated the trade. The fruit trade was also important.

In Soviet times the main elements of the employment structure of the Muslim population remained. The Tatars in Moscow traditionally were engaged in the fur craft, tincture of fur and leather, and were occupied with state trade and service (yard-keepers, waiters). They also worked at mills and factories; the Tatars and the Azerbaidjanis of state institutions had a certain rank amidst Moscow intellectuals including scientific workers. Many of the Azerbaidjanis permanently living in Moscow took control of the vegetable, fruit and flower trades on Moscow markets. This occupation with traditional crafts and trades probably explains the preponderance of technical and secondary education among the Tatars and Azerbaidjanis rather than higher education.[3]

Thus within the limits of the large Russian town there was an equilibrium in the social roles of the representatives of different groups (including the Muslim ones).

Recently under the conditions of a developing market economy, sharpening ethnic and confessional conflicts and the stream of migrants from the Caucasus and the Central Asia caused by those factors, the situation has abruptly changed. The equilibrium of social roles was disturbed, as a regrouping of the employment structure of the stable Muslim population occurred. The market for domestic goods (also from the Caucasus and the Central Asia) came under pressure from imported food products and clothes, and within the traditional Caucasus fruit trade (today mainly in imported fruit) an underground drugs trade came into existence.

The expansion of criminal structures is developing against a background of 'returning to ethnicity' as a primordial and stable basis of personality, contrary to virtues acquired in social life. The search for national and confessional identification, as well as the outburst of confessional and ethnic hostility, are caused by many factors: the unsettled state of most people in the face of a radical breakdown in socio-economic conditions, spiritual and ideological reference points; the aspiration to find ties of solidarity within the definite ethnic group which can provide social and political status and institutionalise clan ties and links of relationship. But at the same time this resurrects the primordial archetypal opposition of 'us' and 'them'.

Socio-economic difficulties and discontent can easily provoke ethnic and confessional hostility, leading to the propagation of negative images of the representatives of another group or confession who in calmer times were treated more charitably. These considerations are confirmed by research carried out at the end of 1992 by the Centre for Public Opinion Studies of Moscow State University.[4]

The subjects of research were 447 Muscovites of ten nationalities: Russians, Ukrainians, Jews, Tatars, Armenians, Mordvinians, Azerbaidjanis, Georgians, Uzbeks and Letts. The information of the 1989 general census of the population, which gives figures for the national structure of Moscow residents, underlay the sample. The Russians, the Ukrainians, the Jews and the Tatars are the most numerous ethnic groups in Moscow. The results of the public opinion poll sometimes testify to inter ethnic tension and mutual antipathy.

In terms of educational qualifications the community with the largest numbers in higher education are the Uzbeks (80 per cent) followed by the Mordvinians (78 per cent), the Jews (77 per cent), the Russians (68 per cent), and the Armenians (67 per cent). The lowest index of higher education is among the Azerbaidjanis (37 per cent) and the Tatars (27 per cent). At the same time the Azerbaidjanis and the Tatars have the largest numbers in secondary education compared to Muscovites of other nationalities: the Azerbaidjanis 63 per cent and the Tatars 59 per cent.

Respondents were asked their opinions of the educational level of the representatives of different ethnic groups: more than half considered the Jews the most educated and the Tatars and the Gypsies the least educated; only 14 per cent considered the Russians to be well educated. Ethnic rivalry has undoubtedly influenced the respondents opinions in this matter: Moscow Armenians consider the Azerbaidjanis the most uneducated and vice versa.

The poll testifies to the formation in Muscovite public consciousness of stereotypes of the representatives of other groups and of their social and professional niches. And often individual groups are not differentiated, but instead subsumed into some newly created pseudo-superethnos. Thus, particularly in recent years, Muscovites refer to people of vastly different groups – from the Georgians to the Chechens – by the term Caucasians and people of Central Asia by the term Asians. Along with such generalisation the stereotypical notion is being formed about the Russians and the Jews as the major representatives of the scientific and creative intelligentsia, of the employees of state institutions and the higher administrative apparatus. Similarly the opinion is common that Russians, Jews and Tatars are engaged in state trade, Russians and Tatars in the services sector, and Russians, Jews and 'Caucasians' in private trade. The latter are often regarded also as dealers, businessmen and even mafiosi.

It is of interest how, in public consciousness, ethnic groups are differentiated in accordance with material success. In recent years as a market economy has been introduced by the methods of shock therapy, material success has come to be associated in the first place with the concepts of wealth and poverty. In the survey 58 per cent of the respondents believed that some ethnic groups were better off than others, especially the 'Caucasians' (some of the respondents specifically mentioned the Chechens), the Jews and the Russians. However, only the Jews (15 per cent) and the Uzbeks (5 per cent) consider the Russians to be rich. Along with these images of the 'wealthy', respondents to the survey identified the following characteristics as promoting success: slyness (34 per cent), intellect (25 per cent), cruelty (17 per cent), insidiousness, ambition and talent (15 per cent each), industry (12 per cent). Virtues, previously highly estimated, are today of low value: conscientiousness (7 per cent), care (6 per cent), honesty and obedience (5 per cent each), responsibility (4 per cent), good nature (3 per cent).[5]

In recent years, as a result of intensifying national and social contradictions as well as of the breakdown of traditional social and moral ideals and values, problems of ethnic and national as well as confessional identity have arisen. In Russia, ethnicity (nationality) was always ascertained by passport, where the nationality of one or both parents was recorded. However, recently the criteria have diversified, for ethnicity inherited from the parents does not always coincide with self-assessment of ethnicity as a result of education and mode of life. Self-assessments of ethnicity which disagree with passport data are especially frequent in mixed families. Many non-Russian Muscovites feel themselves to be Russians. In the course of the survey it emerged that contradictions between passport record and ethnic self-identification exist among Mordvinians (40 per cent), Jews (31 per cent) and Ukrainians (24 per cent). The Tatars (17 per cent), Azerbaidjanis and Uzbeks (3 per cent each) display the least disagreements.[6]

These figures show an intensive process of assimilation developing in the city, where 89.7 per cent of the population are the Russians, together with signs of reorientation of ethnic self-consciousness. At the same time, among the representatives of Muslim groups the aspiration to retain their ethnic and confessional identity is significantly stronger than in other ethnic groups.

Ethnic and confessional groups of Muslims in Moscow having lost touch with the ethnic environment and culture, afterwards develop under the influence of different ethnic and social, confessional, cultural and psychological, as well as social and political factors. Various factors favour conservation or transformation of ethnic and cultural specificity and of ethnic and confessional self-consciousness.

One can indicate the main factors determining the nature of ethnic and confessional processes: the relationship between the national and the Russian languages and the attitude to the national language; attitudes to mixed marriages, the preservation of ethnic and confessional traditions in family life (national food, national names, the observance of religious solemnities, visiting mosques); the maintenance of the calendar of rites and life cycle ceremonies in a canonic form (weddings, funerals, cutting etc.); active participation in national and Islamic cultures (reading classics of the national culture, study of sacred books, visiting the national theatres, musical performances of the national ensembles and participation in them, participation in the interpretation of Koran and Hadith). Let us consider some of these factors.

Table 2

Attitudes to Language among Muslims in Moscow

Ethnic Group		Regard National Language as Native		Regard Russian as Native	
	Total	Total	%	Total	%
Tatars	157,615	99,252	62.9	58,060	37.1
Azerbaidjanis	20,727	15,253	73.6	5,343	26.4
Uzbeks	9,183	7,005	76.2	2,057	23.8
Ossets	7,270	3,961	54.4	3,187	44.4
Bashkirs	5,417	2,707	49.9	2,388	50.1
Chechens	2,101	1,625	77.3	463	22.7

As a rule, Muslims who have migrated to a Russian town speak two languages, but in this situation of bilingualism the native language performs important ethnic and cultural functions. It becomes the indicator of ethnic affiliation, one of the guarantors of preserving ethnic specificity, family and future generations. At the same time knowledge of Russian is an important route and condition of adaptation in a Russian town, the means of socialisation in different spheres of existence: family life, industry, culture and education, public activity. It is typical for the migrants of the first generation to regard the language of their nationality as a native one while those born in a town consider Russian their native language. But in the circumstances of a 'return to the ethnic', national language becomes the symbol of ethnic self-identification and interest in it grows.

This tendency is shown in efforts to teach children the language of their nationality, to preserve the language tradition in family life, and retain the ability to read and write in the national language.

Table 2, adapted from the 1989 census, illustrates the relationship between the national and the Russian languages among the various groups of Muslims in Moscow.[7] Judging by the linguistic situation among the representatives of the Muslim groups, the most advanced on the path of integration into the Russian majority are the Bashkirs, the Ossets, and the Tatars and the least advanced are the Chechens, the Uzbeks and the Azerbaidjanis. Alongside this, however, there have been increasing attempts to conserve ethnic and confessional specificity.

So, today in Moscow the process of returning to the national language is proceeding. In the course of a limited research project carried out with the author's participation among Tatar children and their parents, it turned out that fathers (who were yard-keepers, carpenters, painters) and mothers (who were kindergarten-nurses, office cleaners) wanted their children to learn the Tatar language, to visit a mosque and a *medresse*. Some of the parents attend lessons in the Tatar language in a mosque. In Moscow the practice of children and adults learning the national language in private schools has become widespread.

An important feature of ethnic relations is mixed marriages and attitudes to them. In the Muslim environment in Moscow the situation is quite specific: among the migrants of the first generation the number of mixed marriages is higher than among the settled Moscow Muslim population. In the course of observations and inquiries it has turned out that indigenous Tatar families in Moscow oppose mixed marriages and prefer not only marriages within the nationality but those between members of the Tatar sub-groups (of Kazan, Siberia, Astrakhan, the Crimea, etc.) and in particular between people of the same ethnic and confessional group. For example, the Tatar Muslims object to marriages with Tatar Kriashens (the baptised Tatars).

In Kazan (Tatarstan) by 1990 the rate of mixed marriages reached almost 30 per cent (65 per cent are marriages between Russians and Tatars) while in Moscow only about 25 per cent of Tatars married people of other nationalities, and in St. Petersburg 26 per cent (40 per cent of them want their children to choose the Tatar nationality). There are considerably more marriages of Muslim men to Russian women (and family attitudes to them are more loyal), than of Muslim women to Russian men. This reflects the *sharia* requirement forbidding Muslim women to marry non-Muslims, while there is no prohibition on the marriage of a Muslim man to a woman of another confession.

Muslim Muscovites are particularly zealous in the preservation of their ethnic and confessional culture. Historically, Moscow was a stronghold of Christian orthodoxy. Its administration was more zealous, as compared with, for example, St Petersburg in putting into practice the Tsarist government's legislative acts restricting the rights of aliens. As a result traditions of close contact, mutual help and support, the preservation of ethnic and confessional specificity and Muslim culture have been established among Muslims in Moscow. Studies on Tatar families have shown that about 80 per cent of the Tatars cook national dishes, half of them several times a week, and others at least at high days and holidays. Among the Tatars 40 per cent have retained articles of ethnic family life: utensils, clothes, adornments. In an inter-ethnic environment in a city there is a stronger preservation of the calendar rites and traditional festivals: *kurban-bayram, uraza, sabantuy*, and old life cycle rites are being performed according to the complete canonical form.

One may notice a certain paradox: indigenous Muslim families, whose history of residence in Moscow numbers several generations, oppose assimilation and preserve their national specificity to a higher degree than Muslim and especially mixed families living in Moscow for 20-30 years.

In recent years on the territory of the former USSR, including Moscow, an interest in Islam and Muslim culture has grown. This phenomenon is closely connected with the return to ethnicity and represents a form of so-called religious nationalism. In connection with the transformation of ethnoses and ethnic self-consciousness in Soviet times, religion, and Islam in particular, came to carry out compensatory and protective functions, opposing dispersion of ethnic specificity and promoting the growth of ethnic and confessional self-consciousness. Under conditions of extremely complicated contradictions, which threaten to ruin former ideals and values, the Muslim Muscovite finds spiritual support and hope in joining one of the world religions, namely Islam. Identification with the world community of Islam provides a sense of self-respect and participation in a source of spiritual values.

For these groups Islam has become not only the basis of acquiring ethnic and confessional self-consciousness, but also of self-organisation and realisation of public and political activity. Since the end of the 1980s a number of unions and movements of 'national and

confessional' orientation have begun to come into being on the basis
of Islam. Such unions, which have appeared both in Moscow and the
new states, serve public, political, cultural and other functions. In the
new states they are regarded as departments, acting on behalf of their
communities.[8] Among such unions it is necessary to mention the
Islamic Revival Party, which has branches in other regions of the former
USSR and combines in its activity public and enlightening elements.
Its leaders, Amir Akhmad-kadi Aktaev and Executive Committee
member Gheidar Jamal, said in an interview to the magazine *The
Elements* that the party considered it necessary to attain stable
consensus between Orthodox and Muslim believers in opposing
Americanisation and in restoring the unity of the state.

There is also the Islamic Centre in Moscow, headed by the imam-
khatib of Moscow Cathedral Mosque Sheikh Ravil Ghainoutdyn. The
Centre promotes the following objectives: popularisation of Muslim
spiritual values, study of the Arab language, Islamic traditions and
culture, the building and reconstruction of mosques and the setting
up of a library and a lecture room. The Centre has set up relations
with scientific organisations studying Islam in Moscow and Damascus,
with Islamic centres in Finland and Germany, and with the Tatar
Association in the USA. It conducts large-scale work, and a Charitable
Fund of the Islamic Centre 'Moscow – Saudi Arabia' has been set up.
There are also national Tatar, Azerbaidjani, Uzbek and Chechen
centres in Moscow. The Tatar Public Centre is a large and influential
public and political union. The Centre carries out its activities
throughout the territory of the former USSR, maintains close contacts
with the Tatar diaspora. Groups of Tatars Kriashens, a group of
Crimean Tatars, and a group of the Azerbaidjanis are represented in
the Centre in the form of sections. The programme of the Centre
envisages ensuring the sovereignty of the Tatars, reaching national
consolidation, cultural and linguistic reunification of all the Tatar
groups, development of spiritual culture, Muslim enlightenment and
education of the Tatars.

The league of the Tatar young people 'Azatlik' has been founded as
a youth wing of the Tatar Public Centre. The radical wing of the
Tatar Public Centre has been transformed into the Tatar Party of
National Independence 'Ittifak'. In 1992 the People's Democratic Party
'Vatan' was set up in Moscow, with the goal of bringing about the
cultural and national revival of the Tatar nation on the basis of Islam.

The youth centre of Muslim culture 'Iman' was founded at the initiative of the Muslim cultural centre in Moscow. Its task is 'study, development and dissemination of Muslim spiritual and cultural values to solve the problems of humanitarian and social-economic perfection of human beings'. It stresses an aspiration for 'consolidation of efforts of Muslim youth, students and intelligentsia, including the Muslim clergy, representatives of culture, science, mass media and public figures, for all round revival of the Muslim spiritual heritage.'

'Pure Islam' is a small inward looking group which regards itself as representing true Islam. It has sections in Moscow, Kazan, St. Petersburg, and Tashkent. The movement advocates the idea of the only true path on earth, the path of the Koran. All those who do not follow it are 'lost people'. The state must provide facilities for Moslem prayer, for the teaching of the principles of Islam and for the propagation of the Moslem doctrine.

Notes

1. *Narodnoe khozyaystvo v SSSR v 1990 godu. Statisticheski ezhegodnik.* Moscow, 1991 (National Economy in the USSR in 1990. Statistical Annual).
2. *Raspredelenie nasseleniya po natsionalnosti, rodnomu yazyku i vtoromu yazyku narodov SSSR. Itogi perepissi nasseleniya 1989 goda.* Moscow 1989 (Distribution of the Population by Nationality, Native Language, the Second Language of the Peoples of the USSR. The 1989 Census Results).
3. *Nekotorye pokazateli, kharakterizuyushchie natsionalnyi sostav nasseleniya Rossiyskoi Federatsii (po dannym perepissi nasseleniya 1989 goda).* T.III, Ch.I i II. Moscow 1993 (Some Indicators Characterising the National Composition of the Population of the Russian Federation (by the 1989 Census Data).
4. Belyaeva G., Dragunski D., Zotova L. 'Mnogonatsionalnyi Mir Moskvy (The multinational world of Moscow)', *Druzhba narodov,* 1993, No.4, pp.134-48.
5. Ibid.
6. Ibid.
7. *Raspredelenie nasseleniya.*
8. Iskhakov D.M. 'Neformalnye obyedineniya v sovremennom tatarskom obshchestve', *Sovremennye natsionalnye protsessy v Respublike Tatarstan,* Kazan 1992, pp.5-51. ('Informal associations in contemporary Tartar society', in *Contemporary National Processes in the Republic of Tatarstan.*)

9

Muslim Immigrant Communities and Foreign Policy in Western Europe

Jørgen S. Nielsen

For countries of Western Europe, the presence of a permanently resident Muslim minority is a comparatively recent phenomenon, as distinct from Eastern Europe where there have been substantial Muslim communities for centuries. This new presence is one which the various countries are only gradually beginning to learn to live with.

Having called these communities Muslim it is, of course, clear that they are by no means homogeneous. They originate from a variety of countries in Asia, Africa and the Americas. While most come from small village backgrounds, they also include professionally and technically educated people and small and large businessmen. Their children are increasingly born and brought up in Europe with only passing contact, if at all, with the country of origin. For many, Islam is mostly an aspect of their culture with a minimum of religious practice and commitment. But others have a religious commitment and regularly practice some or all of their religious duties – and these are certainly a much higher proportion than the equivalent among European Christians. Almost inevitably, this religious commitment leads to further divisions as people ally themselves with different mosques and different religious trends.

Common to all the communities is, however, not only their Islam but also that they are essentially the product of European empires. The three main countries of Western European immigration have been Britain, France and West Germany. Britain's immigrant population came from its former colonies in the Caribbean and the

Indian subcontinent, and France's from North and West Africa. Germany's came from Turkey with which the country had had both political and economic relations not dissimilar to those of empire. The smaller countries around Western Europe tended to follow the lead of the 'big three' when they also started looking for immigrant labour.]

France is now the country with the largest Muslim population, over three million, two thirds of whom are from the three Arab North African countries of Algeria, Morocco and Tunisia, with one million alone from Algeria. In addition there are large numbers of Turks and West Africans. The Muslim population of Germany counts about 1.8 million 1.5 of which are Turks or Kurds from Turkey. The figure in Britain is over one million, two thirds of whom originate in the Indian subcontinent either directly or indirectly via East Africa; Pakistanis are the single largest group. Other smaller groups come from the Arab world, Iran, sub-Saharan Africa and Turkish Cyprus. In the Netherlands there are about 150,000 each of Turks and Moroccans with another 100,000 of various origins including the Indian subcontinent making a total of about 400,000. About half of the 300,000 Muslims in Belgium have come from Morocco, a quarter from Turkey and the rest from other parts of North and West Africa. Italy has approximately the same total as Belgium with Arabs from North Africa and the Middle East predominant. The Spanish Muslim population is almost impossible to assess due to a high rate of illegal residents, but estimates are in the region of a quarter million with Moroccans the largest group. Sweden, Switzerland and Austria each have about 100,000, in all three cases mostly Turks. Denmark has a population of some 60,000 consisting especially of Iranians, Arabs, Turks and Pakistanis. Norway's 40,000 Muslims come from Turkey and Morocco.[1]

As a result of this process Western Europe today has between eight and ten million people who are Muslim in some sense. Most of them are perceived as being foreigners, even though a substantial proportion have become citizens of their new countries. There remain very lively connections with the countries of origin and the extended families there. As a new generation born in Europe reaches adulthood, these connections are tending to weaken, but this is accompanied by a growing interest in events among the Muslim community worldwide, especially among those sections of the young who are actively Muslim.]

It is inconceivable that communities totalling almost twice the population of Denmark, concentrated in major cities, and with strong family, community and cultural ties outside Europe should not at some stage begin to affect European foreign policy. The question is whether they have already done so, how such influence might come about and be directed, and how European governments and public opinion perceive and react to this new situation.

There have been several instances in the past which might justify consideration. Before the era of large scale immigration the Paris Mosque and then the London Central Mosque were established with government support. The Paris Mosque was opened in 1929 in recognition of the part troops from French North Africa had played in the 1914–18 war, and at a time when some sectors of North African society were beginning to show restiveness at French rule.[2] The London Central Mosque was given its present site in 1944 by the government in exchange for a site in Cairo for the Anglican cathedral but also, one suspects, with an eye to the participation of Indian colonial troops in the 1939–45 war and the growing independence movement in India.[3]

At the time of these two cases, there were certainly Muslims in each of the two countries, probably substantially more in France than in Britain. Both governments were under some lobbying pressure from leading members of those communities, but the pressure would only have been credible because of the foreign policy needs of the time. These measures, therefore, could more correctly be described as domestic actions taken in the light of foreign policy considerations, the reverse of what we are looking for. The establishment of a cemetery and mosque in Berlin in 1866 was primarily a symptom of the deepening commercial and political relationships between Prussia/Germany and the Ottoman Empire.

It is really only with the arrival and settlement of Muslim communities during the 1950s and 1960s that the possibility arises of domestic Muslim influence on foreign policy. The first case which might be considered is that of the Belgian decision in 1974 to extend to Islam the recognition which was already accorded to Catholics, Protestants, Anglicans and Jews. This was at a time when Muslim immigrants counted between 70 and 80,000 almost double the number of Protestants. Although the first proposal to extend recognition had been made in 1971, the context of the decision was clearly that of the

1972–74 oil crisis and the attempts by Arab states to use oil as a political weapon after the October 1973 Arab–Israeli war.[4] The Belgian move must therefore be judged to have been made in response to perceived foreign pressures and for foreign policy purposes, even though overwhelmingly with reference to domestic Muslim communities.

One must probably judge in a similar manner the Italian decision in the late 1970s to give political support to the building of the great mosque in Rome, a decision which was announced in the context of a visit by the Italian prime minister to Saudi Arabia.

In the period roughly between these two events, i.e. in the late 1970s, a much more complex development was taking place between West Germany and Turkey, in which Muslim organisations were playing a significant part. During the growing crisis of authority in Turkey in this period, it was evident that various factions campaigning underground against the Turkish authorities were mobilising and finding significant support among Turkish immigrants, especially those in Germany. This applied to radical leftist factions bridging the Turkish–Kurdish divide, as well as Kurdish nationalist groups, and included Marxist and communist groups. It also applied to the Islamist opposition who opposed the strict Kemalist heritage of the 1920s and were not satisfied with the compromises entered into since the 1940s. These groups ranged from comparatively moderate trends to extreme right-wing tendencies for whom Islamism was subservient to extreme Turkish nationalism. The Iranian revolution in 1979 encouraged Islamist trends.

The military coup of September 1980 led directly to a change of policy towards Islamic organisations coordinated between Ankara and Bonn. With the active agreement of Bonn, the Turkish government set about asserting its control over the Turkish Muslim organisations in Germany. The main instrument was the Department of Religious Affairs (commonly known as the Diyanet) in the Prime Minister's Office. The German authorities agreed with Turkey that only imams and religious teachers approved by the Diyanet would be allowed to enter Germany to serve in mosques, and then only for a limited period, usually five years. In 1981, the Diyanet set up an office with the status of foundation in Cologne, known from its Turkish initials as DITIB. Through this office the Diyanet successfully expanded its influence among Turkish Muslim communities, so much so that by the end of the 1980s it was estimated that between half and two-thirds of Turkish mosques in Germany were linked to the Diyanet.[5]

The effect of these developments has been to neutralise any impact that the Turkish Muslim presence in Germany might have had on the country's policy towards Turkey. In any event such impact would have been weak, given that every effort has been taken by the German authorities to minimise the possibility of Turkish immigrants becoming German citizens and thus take part in the German political process from within. It would seem that Ankara during the 1980s considered it a priority to stop the Turks in Germany from again becoming a base for opposition activity. It certainly does not appear to have viewed them as a potential pressure point to persuade Germany to change its attitude to, for example, Turkey's application for membership of the European Union. This is in sharp contrast to the role the Catholic church would appear to have played in persuading Bonn to press for the European recognition of Croatia and Slovenia in 1992.

There are a number of other instances of Muslim immigrant communities playing a significant role as a safe haven or strategic base for opposition politics in the countries of origin. During the Algerian war of independence, the French authorities realised that Algerians in metropolitan France were a major source of support for the uprising – at times as many as ten thousand Algerians in France were being held in custody to try to neutralise this support. It has sometimes been stated that much of the external support for the Muslim Brotherhood's uprising in Syria 1979–81 was coordinated through the Islamic Cultural Centre in Aachen, Germany. The degree of effective involvement has probably been exaggerated, although the network around this centre and others in Germany can be assumed to have provided 'safe houses' and other forms of support both to the Syrian opposition and to other exile political groups. Other small sectors of the foreign community, often linked to German underground groups, clearly provided similar services for terrorist groups operating in the Middle East.

There remain four cases which potentially match what we are looking for, namely instances where a European foreign policy has been influenced by a resident minority of foreign origin. These are the Rushdie affair, the Gulf war, the Bosnian war, and the Islamic uprising in Algeria.

We have to distinguish two separate dimensions of the Rushdie affair. The first was the domestic agenda, the campaign by various Muslim groups in Britain to have Salman Rushdie's The Satanic Verses banned or withdrawn from the market. This started as soon as the book was published, although it hardly drew public attention until a public burning of the book by demonstrators in Bradford in January 1989, four months after publication. The attention of a number of Muslims governments had been drawn to the anti-Islamic nature of the book by several British Muslim organisations. But it was only after the second dimension was introduced that there was a foreign policy impact. This was when Ayatollah Khomeini in February 1989 issued a fatwa calling for the death of the author.[6]

At this point the implications of the affair became international in nature, but only in Britain was there a significant continuing link between the domestic and the international dimensions. It is to be noted that, with a very few exceptions, Muslim communities in Western European countries kept a very low profile regarding Rushdie's book in its various translations and that most distanced themselves from the fatwa. The fatwa provoked a renewed crisis between Western European states and Iran, but the crisis was complicated by at least initial uncertainties regarding how other Muslim states were going to react. In the event it transpired that the fatwa had political targets additional to and to some extent more important than the ostensible one: it was part of both a domestic Iranian process and of a wider regional process. So while Britain broke off diplomatic relations and other countries froze or downgraded theirs, the solution to the fatwa crisis was really outside the control of the European foreign ministries. In the meanwhile, in Britain the domestic campaign and response continued although greatly distracted by the Iranian dimension. Although this campaign did not achieve its direct aims, it did result in a much greater public awareness of the domestic Muslim community. This was often negative in character but at the same time both central and local government started taking the Muslim communities and their aspirations more seriously, and various informal and formal means were used to establish and maintain contact.

Eighteen months later the still simmering affair was pushed out of the public's attention by Iraq's invasion of Kuwait. Once it became clear that Britain, France and other European countries in various ways were preparing to participate in the military effort to reverse the

Iraqi action, appeals to Islamic solidarity and rectitude were launched by both Iraq and its Middle Eastern opponents. Iraq threatened to mobilise terror squads against its enemies. Khomeini had made similar threats against Salman Rushdie, but then the reactions of the authorities had been low-profile, although one can be certain that the intelligence services were active. The reaction on this occasion, however, was much more forthright.

In both Britain and France, the two main countries involved, hundreds of perceived 'security risks' were taken into custody. France banned Arabic newspapers considered to be supportive of Iraq, including the mainly Palestinian al-Quds al-'Arabi published in London. There were press reports that the French government were worried about the domestic Muslim reaction to its policy, and some were wanting the policy to be trimmed to take that into account. In Britain the media were almost unanimously in support of the government and the only dissent was to be found among small sectors of the political left, the churches and the Muslim communities. Almost inevitably it was the Muslim dissenters who had to face the accusation of disloyalty. As in the Rushdie affair this spilled over into the domestic race relations scene, adding further to the growing number of young Muslims looking for ways of becoming politically active. This was the time when the UK Muslim Parliament was being established, and the UK Islamic Party started presenting candidates for election to local councils. In the event neither have been particularly successful, but they are symptomatic of a trend.

In both the Rushdie affair and the Gulf war the Muslim communities in Western Europe had shown indications of what might have been. Significant sections were opposed to what their governments were doing. But while government officials were expressing a concern that their domestic Muslim communities might be used by foreign states to apply domestic pressure, there is no evidence that such pressure had any effect, except perhaps in minor matters where decisions might have been taken to pre-empt a perceived pressure. Indeed, there is little evidence of such pressure being attempted, the loud proclamations from Baghdad and other capitals notwithstanding. Another reason for the lack of effective pressure was clearly the fact that there was no united Muslim voice.

In the case of the war in Bosnia, there is little doubt that the Muslim communities across Europe are united in their views. But this case illustrates well the fact that foreign policy is only rarely influenced directly by the pressures of domestic public opinion. The Muslim support of the Bosnian government cause is complemented by a widespread general public opinion disgusted and frustrated by Serb actions. But this combination has had minimal effect on government policies. Both Paris and London, each in their own way, have concentrated their practical intervention on the humanitarian plane and only in extreme cases endorsed direct military intervention. Policy towards the crisis as a whole appears to have been determined more by concern to keep Russia from breaking ranks and to avoid delegating real foreign policy decision-making to the European Commission in Brussels. The coincidence of opinion between the USA and European Muslims in favour of a suspension of the arms embargo on the Bosnian government has not moved Europe's capitals.

Finally, the case of Franco–Algerian relations after the annulment of the general elections in 1992 must be considered briefly. The rise of the Front Islamique de Salut (FIS) in the context of a general deterioration of the social and economic situation in Algeria started worrying France from the mid-1980s. A particular aspect of French concern must be the fact that Islamism is there seen against a backdrop of almost ideological republican laicism which was cemented into French law by legislation in 1905. One strong element of this laicism, arising out of the particular circumstances leading to the 1905 legislation, is an undercurrent of anticlericalism which continues occasionally to be expressed explicitly in face of its traditional target, the Roman Catholic church. Against this backdrop, a public expression of religious agendas in political debate registers with relatively more force, by shear contrast, than it often does in other European countries. Already in the mid-1980s, the spreading influence of the movement Foi et pratique was making many normally relaxed French observers worried, even though Foi et pratique was an almost integral part of the Tablighi Jamaat movement, a pietistic and, above all, politically quietist, movement of Indian subcontinent origin.

The 'headscarves affair' of September 1989[7], with its much wider context of French reactions to Middle Eastern inspired terrorism and the bicentennial celebrations of the French Revolution, served to disproportionately heighten public consciousness of possible issues at stake. The fear of possibly growing immigration pressures – in France obviously perceived as coming from the south – was linked to the growing support for FIS in Algeria, expressed initially in widespread local election successes. As the general election in Algeria approached and seemed to promise a FIS victory, French public debate and discussion among academics (in France always much more publicly displayed in the broadcast and print media than in most of the rest of Europe) began to build up to a hitherto unprecedented level of tension. There was almost a collective sigh of relief when the Algerian military command pushed the election process aside at the last minute. What has happened since then both in Algeria and in French policy towards Algerians in France, especially several waves of collective arrests of allegedly Islamic militants, has merely served to confirm what amounts to an official French laager-mentality: all active Muslims in France, whatever their programme, are actual or potential FIS-activists, with no reference to any of the wide variety of opinion as to goal and method which such a global term might cover.

Clearly, the relevant French authorities have been displaying not only an inept refusal to recognise that Muslim opinion is not monolithic but also an aspect of traditional European racism and xenophobia. But the issues have also been caught up in internal political contests, where the growing electoral threat of the Front National of Le Pen has encouraged the parties of the centre–right (essentially the heirs of de Gaulle) to compete for the same vote.

On balance it would seem that it is government authorities in France which have hitherto displayed the most nerves about the possibility of Muslim minorities within Europe's boundaries playing the role of a 'fifth column' in favour of a foreign power. Some of that can be attributed to the country's vicinity to the Muslim world in North Africa (but why does one not see an even stronger fear on this count from Spain?), and much can, in my view, be attributed to the contrast which any kind of religio-political involvement presents to the ideological, and basically anti-clericalist, laicism of the French Republic.

Considering these four candidates as possible case studies for our overall thesis, I find myself reaching the conclusion that the case remains unproven. There may be elements of ethnic and national interests in certain cases, but Islam would seem so far to be a contributory factor rather than at the core. Where Islam does appear to attain some significance it is in the perceptions of the 'host' government rather than in fact – dare one suggest here a degree of paranoia?

But the only conclusion this can lead one to is that Muslim minorities in Europe have not hitherto and in themselves been an influence on European foreign policy. This does not justify a conclusion that there is no such potential in the future, and possibly the near future at that.

It might therefore be useful to look at the possible ways and means by which such a relationship between Muslim domestic minorities and foreign policy could become effective. There are two elements to this. Firstly, we have to identify different categories of movements in terms of their aims and the role that European Muslim minorities might play in the achievement of those aims. Secondly, we need to consider more closely the role that funding links plays.

It is possible to identify four categories of Islamic movements in Europe for the purposes of this analysis:

A. Some are sponsored by the governments of the countries of origin. We have already mentioned earlier the relationship between the Turkish government's religious office, Diyanet, and its subsidiary in Cologne, DITIB. This channels staff to German mosques and some funding. But the personnel link is the most significant, and by the policy of regular five-yearly rotation of appointments Ankara minimises the potential for a German-based religious leadership with its own priorities. In a different fashion the Moroccan Amicales des ouvriers et commerçants operating especially in France, where it was founded in 1973, Belgium and the Netherlands preserve the link between the Moroccan monarchy and emigré Moroccans, although in this case without the cooperation of the host governments. That the link nevertheless is powerful has been illustrated by the situation in the Netherlands. Here foreigners may vote in and stand as candidates for local elections. On the first occasion this was allowed, a significant number of Moroccan immigrants were nominated for election. Shortly before the election itself, the Moroccan authorities let it be known that they did not want Moroccans taking part in the Dutch electoral process with the result that a large proportion of the candidates withdrew their nominations and most Moroccans did not vote. It was notable that Moroccan and Turkish participation in demonstrations against Salman Rushdie was almost non-existent.

It seems reasonable to conclude that movements of this nature exist primarily in the interests of the governments of the countries of origin. Their purpose is to retain support and minimise opposition by controlling as far as possible their expatriates in Europe. In the case of Germany and Turkey, the host country cooperates in this process in a way that many other host governments have rejected. Sweden has been particularly consistent in refusing to cooperate with sending countries in regulating the appointment of mother tongue teachers or imams, choosing to fund both from the Swedish public purse.

B. Some groups remain apolitical, choosing to concentrate their efforts on recruiting, servicing and retaining their supporters. Although apolitical their activities tend to be in areas of some importance for the Muslim community, e.g. social welfare, education, and the encouragement of personal and collective piety. Their involvement in the politics of either country of origin or of settlement is minimal if not non-existent. When there is involvement it is usually primarily to defend their own freedom to function. The network of the Tablighi-jamaat is a prime example of this, although it has to be noted that the Algerian part of the movement has become politically active as one of the coalition of movements in FIS; it is not clear how far the related French Foi et pratique has also changed character.

C. Some movements clearly have a political agenda but it relates primarily to its own role in the country of origin, its international networks, and its relations with other similar movements. Many Sufi-based organisations, tariqas, can be identified in this category. Some of the West African, especially Senegalese, and Indian subcontinent tariqas have been quietly, in recent years not so quietly, expanding their following among the emigré populations. For a long time in Britain they were almost invisible, and outside observers assumed that the Sufi tradition was dying with the migration. In the early to mid-1980s they started again to become visible, partly because a few scholars who had the experience to recognise what they saw entered the field,[8] and partly because they began to take on a British organisational form. They are today clearly one of the most significant factors in the community life of Muslims of Indian subcontinent origin. Their involvement in British politics is primarily at the local level and aimed almost exclusively at improving their own circumstances. In France West African tariqas, always more tightly organised than their subcontinent counterparts, had also passed virtually unnoticed until they suddenly came to prominence during the motor industry strikes, where they effectively set up their own trade union branches inside the communist union federation.[9] While both groups of Sufi networks retain strong and lively links between their European bases and the countries of origin, their political agendas have no connection to the foreign policies of the countries of settlement.

D. A very few groups are explicitly political in character. In these cases the question has to be asked: where is their political horizon? In almost all cases it relates to the country of origin. This is the situation where the European settlers are perceived as support structures away from the control of the government and official restrictions of the countries of origin. This is the phenomenon with which a country like Turkey has sought to come to grips in its religious policy in Germany. But such opposition groups based on Islamic programmes do not differ in this respect from a host of other opposition groups, be they Turkish Kurds in Sweden, or Iraqi opposition groups in London. They may be more likely to find support if there is a numerically strong settler population with shared sympathies, such as Kashmiris in Britain. But whatever the circumstances, their impact on government policies has been much more crucial for the governments of the countries of origin than of those of settlement. In the latter, the challenges raised have arguably more often been ones of internal security than of anything else.

Referring to these four categories I do not wish to deny that they have had an impact, but I would suggest that where that impact has been felt most has been partly on the foreign policies of the countries of origin and, above all, on the domestic policies of the countries of settlement, both locally and nationally.

The second element which needs to be considered briefly is that of funding, mainly because it is often in public opinion a major source of concern.

While there is undoubtedly a degree of dependence on the part of many organisations on outside funding, the extent of this has been exaggerated. With the passage of time, the extent of such funding is, in any event, falling. Increasingly mosques are being bought or built with the community's own resources. As a younger generation of imams are slowly beginning to appear, they are often part-time or voluntary.

Apart from the few organisations which are in practice government agencies, such as DITIB in Germany, there is also a large question mark against the influence that funding can buy in practice. Although the Saddam Hussein Mosque in Birmingham was built with Iraqi funding, only the name remains as a trace of the Iraqi connection. The Islamic Foundation outside Leicester has intermittently been accused of acting for Saudi Arabia. It has certainly received funding from Saudi Arabia (as has my own centre), but if there is any similarity of views to be detected this is because of a harmony of approaches which is the cause of funding support rather than its consequence. And after an initial phase of cooperation between the Muslim College in London (funded by the Libyan based Islamic Call Society) and networks of mainly Brelwi organisations, this relationship broke down over the 'Rushdie affair'. During the Gulf war some Saudi agencies discovered that the funding or manpower they had provided, and in some cases still were providing, was powerless to prevent general British Muslim antagonism to the Saudi role in the defeat of Iraq.

Considering these various elements I find myself having to reach the interim conclusion that any impact of the Muslim minorities in Europe on European foreign policy has been minimal. Arguably when there has been an impact it has, in any event, not been on a Muslim agenda, but rather a narrowly national or ethnic one. In fact, the political impact of the Muslim minorities in Europe has been significant but primarily in various aspects of domestic policy: local government, education, health, social welfare, etc.

However, this is no indication of future potentials. It does, in fact, seem highly probable that in the medium to long term European Muslims will have an influence on foreign policy, directly through lobbying and campaigning or indirectly as part of the general public opinion. This development will come about as an ever larger proportion of the Muslim communities in Europe become European. Already today about one half of the Muslims of Britain are British born. Over this and the next generation their links to the realities of their countries of origin will be weakening. Some are likely to develop an identification with an almost mythical conception of their countries of origin. Others more consciously Muslim are likely to strengthen their identification with specifically Muslim causes. Doubtless the former do have the potential of being mobilised by parties in the country of origin to put pressure on the host government – which should not come as a surprise, since it was a similar policy the European powers used with minorities in the Ottoman Empire against Istanbul. The latter are more likely to be an influence for balance and moderation on European governments, producing pressure towards a more constructive policy towards the Muslim world; they are also unlikely to be available to particular Muslim governments as a 'fifth column', simply because of their very critical stance towards the Islamic nature of virtually every Muslim government.

Notes

1.   For details see J. S. Nielsen, *Muslims in Western Europe* (2nd ed. Edinburgh: Edinburgh University Press, 1995).
2.   For a history of the Paris mosque, see Alain Boyer, *L'Institut Musulman de la Mosquée de Paris* (Paris: CHEAM, 1992).
3.   The background to the London Central Mosque and Islamic Cultural Centre can be found in M. M. Ally, *History of Muslims in Britain* (unpublished MA thesis, University of Birmingham, 1981).
4.   Chapter 3, F. Dassetto and A. Bastenier, *L'Islam Transplanté* (Antwerp: EPO, 1984); English translation in *idem*. 'The Organisation of Islam in Belgium', *Research Papers: Muslims in Europe*, no.26 (June 1985).
5.   J.Blaschke, 'Islam und Politik unter türkische Arbeitsmigranten', *Jahrbuch zur Geschichte und Gesellschaft des Vorderen und Mittleren Orients, 1984* (Berlin: Express, 1985), 295-366; Klaus Kreiser, 'Die Religionspolitik der Türkei im Jahre 1985', in J. Lähnemann (ed.), *Erziehung zur Kulturbegegnung* (Hamburg: EBV-Rissen, 1986), 216–29.
6.   For details of the affair see Malise Ruthven, *A Satanic Affair: Salman Rushdie and the Rage of Islam* (London: Chatto and Windus, 1990).
7.   For a summary of this see Nielsen, op.cit., 162–4.
8.   A good example of this kind of scholarship is to be found in P.Werbner, 'Sealing the Quran - Offering and sacrifice among Pakistani labour migrants', *Cultural Dynamics*, vol.1, no.1 (1988), 77–97, and in numerous of her other writings; also in P. Lewis, *Islamic Britain: Religion, Politics and Identity among British Muslims* (London: I. B.Tauris, 1994).
9.   René Mouriaux and Catherine Withol de Wenden, 'French trade unionism and Islam', *Research Papers: Muslims in Europe*, no.36 (December 1987).

Islamic Fundamentalism and the Construction of the Self in Post-Modern Society

Peter Clarke

In studies of religious fundamentalism there is a tendency to stress its anti-modern and anti-post modern character and even to see these oppositions as being of its essence. (Caplan, 1987). The term fundamentalism was first applied in the 1920s in the United States to those Christians that considered it a basic duty to wage war on modernising trends in theology in particular and, more generally, against all secularising trends. This, however, is to interpret fundamentalism as simply reactive, whereas the underlying principle is that it affirms that a faith is to be upheld in its literal and complete form, and that a faith really does mean what it says. For this reason fundamentalism is often dismissed by modernists as blind and devoid of any solid intellectual foundations. In its late 18th and 19th-century form what came to be known as fundamentalism was virtually identical with evangelicalism, grounded as it was on the belief that the Bible was authoritative and reliable in history and science as well as in everything else and on the conviction that there was a need for regeneration (for being 'born again') in order to be saved. Fundamentalism was totally opposed to evolutionary theory, maintaining that the Biblical account of creation was indisputably correct, and to all theological speculation of a liberal kind.

Dispensationalism and *separatism* emerged as key doctrines of fundamentalism in the first half of the twentieth century as it moved away from evangelicalism. *Dispensationalism* contained a number of ideas, including the notion of the inerrant nature of the Bible in historical and scientific detail and the understanding that history was divided into seven eras each one marking a different relationship between God and humanity, and that the last dispensation would be the millennium or reign of Christ for a period of one thousand years in Jerusalem. This reign that would be preceded by, among other things, a seven-year period of wars among those who remained on earth after Christ's true followers had been taken up to meet him prior to his full return. *Separatism* was the doctrine that authentic believers should not mix with the 'heretics' and 'apostates' of the main denominations nor, in the teaching of hard-line fundamentalism, with those fundamentalists who associated with non-fundamentalists.

The life style of such fundamentalism was to be marked by spiritual exercises including the daily reading of the Bible, daily prayer, the avoidance of all worldly pleasures, the wearing of sober and modest clothing, the shunning of Christians from the major denominations, which were branded as apostates, and a zeal for mission and evangelisation. There was also a strong commitment to penal reform, the abolition of the slave trade, and to sabbatarian and temperance legislation. This social action was inspired by the belief that a Christian must work constantly for the reform of society in anticipation of the return of Jesus at the start of the millennial age which would witness the triumph of the Gospel throughout the world.

Tensions heightened within fundamentalism and between fundamentalists and evangelicals over the question of the degree of separation that should obtain between fundamentalists and others, hard-line fundamentalists insisting that there should be no association or co-operation between fundamentalists and other Christian denominations, a prescription that Billy Graham among others was to ignore.

Once progressive in the field of social reform, fundamentalists have developed in more recent times a strong conservative involvement in politics in the United States, seen in the activities of the so-called moral majority which arose in the late 1970s and which supported much of the conservative legislation of the Reagan administration.

The above brief outline of the history and main beliefs of fundamentalism offers some indication as to why there is a wide-ranging debate as to whether such a 'Christian' term can meaningfully be applied to Islam. Sayyid Hossein Nasr is among those who believe it should not be so used for, as he states, it is 'most unfortunate and misleading because the term is drawn from the Christian context where it has quite a different connotation'. (1984: 279–80). Nasr makes the important point that while fundamentalism in Christian religious circles is often traditional, that which is referred to as fundamentalist Islam is often opposed to both the spirit and letter of tradition. (Ibid). Lewis also thinks that the use of the term as applied to Islam is unfortunate and that it can be misleading for the same reason. (Lewis, 1988: 117). However, as Lewis notes, in the sense that fundamentalism insists on the literal divine origin and inerrancy of the Bible the term can be applied by extension to the Muslim understanding of the text of the Qur'an (ibid). For others, among them Fazlur Rahman, the application of this label to Islam is a form of arrogance and cultural imperialism: it imposes what is essentially a Western term on a non-Western belief system and shows a lack of interest in the diversity of cultures and religious traditions, reducing all understanding of these phenomena to a Western understanding (1981:34).

This attitude creates obstacles to Jewish–Christian–Muslim dialogue by conducting the dialogue through Christian concepts such as this and others, including 'salvation', 'redemption' and 'revival'. (Hassan, 1990: 151–6). This is but one example of such Christian (Western) intellectual arrogance and imperialism, in that it is seen as a Christian (Western) endeavour to define other faiths in its own terms. (Hassan, 1990: 151–6).

There are many other reasons why the term fundamentalism as applied to Islam is regarded as unacceptable, including the way it is used judgementally in political discourse and by the media to imply anti-modern, backward looking, irrational, immoderate, extreme, fanatical behaviour and even militancy, violence and terrorism. Moreover, the demands of those Muslim groups so designated are often so variable that they would appear to depend as much on situational factors as on a shared set of beliefs, methods and goals. The differences notwithstanding, almost all Muslim 'fundamentalist' movements are anti-secularist. Furthermore, very few have anything against modernity in itself and make ready use of the most up to date products of science and technology. They are familiar with these technologies because a majority of their activists in Iran and Egypt and other parts of the Muslim world come from the 'modern' middle classes and often with an advanced education in science and technology (Ibrahim, 1980 & 1982; Abrahamian, 1989). There seems to be very little unemployment among 'fundamentalist' activists in Egypt and Iran, and Ergil's study of 'militant' Islam in Turkey provides a very similar picture where background is concerned (1980). It is also worth noting that many of the so-called Muslim fundamentalists have little expertise in theology and tend to be anti-clerical.

Statistical correlations between a certain type of background and militancy, while they do not constitute an explanation, might well support an explanatory hypothesis in terms of relative deprivation. In the Egyptian case, as studied by Ibrahim, all the militants he interviewed came from normal, well integrated families. Taken together with their education and class position, this suggested to him that their involvement in 'fundamentalist' Islam might best be understood if seen in terms of status incongruity: high qualifications, high motivations, but little in the way of political and economic opportunity. Clearly, then, it is not the most economically and politically deprived who gravitate toward militant movements. But whatever the merits of this explanation it would perhaps add something to our understanding of the motivation behind militancy if the concept were to be further unpacked to include ethical, psychological and status deprivation.

There is another intriguing aspect to this question and that is the question why people with identical backgrounds diverge in their biographies, some joining militant Islamic movements while others join militant secular movements. In this paper all of the criticisms made against the use of the term fundamentalism when applied to Islam are taken seriously. However, I still would wish to use it, hopefully in a value neutral sense, with the intention of applying it to second and third generation Muslims in Western Europe. It is here suggested that religious fundamentalism in the sense of following literally the teachings of the Qur'an and the code of behaviour laid down therein is seen by an increasing number of second and third generation Muslim youth in Britain and elsewhere in western Europe as an effective means of creating both a recognisably European form of Islam appropriate to the world in which they live and a sense of self compatible with that world. It is about going back to the past not to avoid the present but to move into it. In this response are to be found the beginnings among Muslims in the West of a self-reflective movement that is at the threshold of what is a post-modernist mode of thinking.

The use of the terms traditional, modern and post-modern pose almost as many problems as the use of the label fundamentalism outside the context of conservative Christianity. Very broadly, in a traditional view of the world one acts according to what the authority of God or the equivalent of God commands; one finds out what role one is to play in the Creator's or Life Force's overall plan, and then one seeks to conform to that role.

The 'modern' mode of thinking is characterised by the belief that the individual is detached from the universe, which is not regarded as the dictator of what is to happen but rather as an instrument or machine. For the modern individual destiny is written in science and/ or technology and not in the stars. In the religious context modernism is about not taking truth at its face value, seeing it as 'symbolic', and the truths of science and religion as constituting separate forms of discourse.

The modern outlook like the traditional outlook is fixed, singular and defensive. It has tended to assume that only one view of reality can be taken at face value, the scientific view. The traditional religious view of reality which science challenged and claimed in so many ways to be false, was also absolutist. It allowed for no alternative version of truth. To take an example, it was not until the 1960s that the Catholic church accepted that its own understanding and presentation of revealed truth could be enhanced by dialogue with other faiths and that the latter could be genuine recipients of that revealed truth. Even today neither Catholicism nor Islam accepts that its version of truth is one alongside others. To adherents who were socialised into the beliefs and practices of these faiths the understanding of the world which they took on was incontrovertible. So incontrovertible that in response to Darwinian evolutionary theory and the claims of positivism, the mirror image of Catholicism in this respect, the dogmas of the immaculate conception and the assumptions were proclaimed at the First Vatican Council towards the end of the nineteenth century.

Post-modernism is not easily defined. While it can mean different things in different spheres of life it always implies heterogeneity, pluralism, permissiveness - not in the sense that people can do as they like but rather in the sense that, for example, they choose their beliefs rather than follow them because of tradition or imposition, and an absence of dogma. In architecture it represents an attempt to describe the move away from modernism which was essentially functionalist and replace it with a more heterogeneous mix of function and value. The emphasis on heterogeneity and the lack of a dominant style are also important elements in post-modern literature, and there is the same reaction against dogma in music.

The post-modernist, by way of contrast with the traditionalist and modernist, sees all systems of ideas and knowledge as starting from a particular set of presuppositions, as founded on a particular set of assumptions, as 'constructs', and all interpretations of reality as interpretations only. It is about how different disciplines and peoples come to interpret reality as much as about their understandings of reality itself. The 'fundamentalists' discussed here have not reached this position as yet but as previously noted are moving in that direction. 'Fundamentalism' needs to be distinguished from 'traditionalism'.

'Traditionalism' like 'fundamentalism' can also be used as a source of innovation, and in the 'traditional' pre-Enlightenment world of Europe it was an indispensable means of political innovation. Even in the post-modern world tradition can be and is used in much the same way. For example, in Japan, the widespread attention to the well-being of the ancestors characteristic of many Japanese new religions is not only symptomatic of a desire to connect with the past but is also a means of ritually closing the door on tradition. Contented ancestors do not make too many serious demands on one's time or interfere with one's progress.

'Traditionalism' exists in every society and is not, as already pointed out, the enemy of modernity although it may oppose modernity where it perceives it to be destructive of what are regarded as important values and traditions. In all societies 'tradition' is made to serve both as a basis of reform and innovation and as a defence of the status quo. There are, however, differences between the importance attached to 'traditionalism' in so called 'traditional' societies and in modern societies. The latter have their own 'traditionalisms' in the fields of science, philosophy and religion, among others, even if these are often brought into play to discredit other kinds of 'traditionalism'. It seems to be the case, however, that in the modern/post-modern world 'traditionalism' is less of a societal force than in, for example, certain Islamic societies where greater value is placed on continuity with traditional norms and practices long ago revealed by God through the Prophet Muhammad. Conversely, in the modern and post-modern world change is desirable in itself.

Because of these and other ambiguities 'traditionalism' is used here in a broad sense to refer to those societal norms and institutions that a culture perceives as congruent with or continuing older precedents and values which are important if not essential to its identity. This definition offers only a limited insight into the nature of Islamic 'traditionalism'. Essentially, as previously noted, this is about the primacy of the authority of the Qur'an and the practice (*sunna*) of the prophet Muhammad in all matters of belief and conduct. And, as in other 'traditionalisms', including Hindu and Sikh versions, there is an important element of 'linking' the present through trustworthy persons across time with the earliest period of Islam, the era of the first four caliphs. For the traditionalist Muslim this person-based link to the ideal Muslim preacher and practitioner and to a model past provides the only sound foundations for self-change and self-development just as it does for social change and development.

Other features of Islamic traditionalism include its 'realism'; it is aware of the departure of the Muslim community from the state of perfection of its very earliest days but does not seek to restore that perfection by revolutionary means. It is reformist rather than radical and militant and does not easily engage in revolution for the purpose of attaining the ends it pursues.

Islamic 'traditionalism' is evolutionist in its understanding of history. The image of the tree with its trunk and branches all interdependent gives an idea of its historical perspective and its attitude to change. By contrast 'fundamentalism's' outlook seeks to ignore history (Tibi, 1992). It is anti-context in its hermeneutics and in its interpretation of history. This paradoxically allows it to embrace the modern, as it does in its acceptance and use of modern science and of modern technology. Moreover, unlike 'traditionalism' it actively promotes Islam as an ideology making for a close similarity between itself and modernism.

This historical, contextual, ideological version of Islam has considerable appeal among second and third generation European Muslims. This is particularly true of European Muslims of South Asian origin who have discovered in it a means both of self-deconstruction (shedding aspects of traditions and cultures they believed were inextricably at one and the same time part of their essential being and of being a Muslim) and of self-construction as a European and a Muslim.

In a community where the vast majority of members are under forty years of age (Nielsen, 1992) the future rests with these young Muslims who are struggling with their dual heritage and are in search of an Islam that will allow them resolve what very often amounts to deep identity crisis. Some of these young Muslims speak of having their feet on two planets, others of planning to return 'home' when they wake up in morning only to have to become accustomed again to Britain or France or Germany by noon, while others write of travelling thousands of miles everyday 'there and back' on an imaginary train, of living between 'wardrobe and suitcase'. The crisis can be extremely painful (Clarke, 1990: 199).

One writes:

> I carry two worlds within me but neither is a whole, they are both bleeding unceasingly, their front line goes through my tongue, I keep picking at it like a prisoner playing on a wound.(ibid)

Such Muslims use the Qur'an to question assumptions concerning what is and what is not Islamic: or more precisely, to question the cultural dimensions of the Islam passed on to them by their parents for the purpose of constructing an Islam more in keeping with their needs and identity as European born and European educated Muslims with a future in a pluralistic European world which they will participate in shaping. This does not mean that in terms of ideas, fashion, diet and leisure pursuits they become similar to other Europeans not of their faith or cultural and racial background. Far from it. The wearing of the head scarf by Muslim women, to take an example, can be a protest against the norms and values of the Western world and the Western attitudes and behaviour of leaders of the Muslim world who condemn the evil consequences of espousing non-Muslim values. Similarly, discarding the head scarf can be a statement to the Muslim community in which they live of their readiness to live by the Qur'an alone and not by customs and traditions that have no basis therein.

By means of this process of returning to the foundations these Muslims are beginning to enter a post-modern stage of thinking not only in terms of Islam itself, in that they acknowledge that their religion can take various forms including a European form, but also in the wider sense of acquiring the capacity to see that there is more than one system of reality. In this respect their fundamentalism is enabling them to move beyond the binary thinking that prevails in 'traditionalist' and modern societies to a post-modern position that refuses to accept that any one interpretation of reality has absolute status. All interpretations are constructs and offer individuals different vehicles for defining and explaining themselves.

References

E. Abrahamian, 'The guerrilla movements in Iran 1963–1977', *MERIP Reports*, No.86, pp. 3–15.

— (1989) , *Radical Islam. The Iranian Mujahedin*, London: I.B.Tauris.

L. Caplan (ed.), (1987), *Religious Fundamentalism*, Houndsmills, Basingstoke: Macmillan.

P .B. Clarke (1990), 'Islam in Contemporary Europe' in, Peter Clarke (ed.), *Islam*, London: Routledge, pp. 192–213.

D. Ergil (1980), *Terrorism and Violence in Turkey*, Ankara.

R. Hassan (1990), 'The Burgeoning of Islamic Fundamentalism: Toward an Understanding of the Phenomenon', in N. J. Cohen (ed.) *The Fundamentalist Phenomenon*, Grand Rapids, Michigan: William B Erdmans, pp. 151–71.

S. E. Ibrahim (1980), 'Anatomy of Egypt's Militant Islamic Groups: Methodological Note and preliminary findings', *International Journal of Middle Eastern Studies*, 12, 423–53.

— (1982), 'Islamic Militancy as a social movement: the case of two groups in Egypt' in A. E. Hillal Dessouki (ed.), *Islamic Resurgence in the Arab World*, New York: Praeger, pp. 117–37.

S. Hossein Nasr (1984), 'Present Tendencies, Future Trends' in M. Kelly (ed.), *Islam: The Religious and Political Life of a World Community*, New York: Praeger.

B. Lewis (1988), *The Political Language of Islam*, Chicago: Chicago University Press.

J. Nielsen (1992), *Muslims in Western Europe*, Edinburgh: Edinburgh University Press.

F. Rahman (1981), 'Roots of Islamic Neo-Fundamentalism' in P. H. Stoddard et al (eds), *Change in the Muslim World*, Syracuse: Syracuse University Press.

B. Tibi (1992), 'Major Themes in the Arabic Political Literature of Islamic Revivalism, 1970–1985: The Islamic System of Government (*al-nizam al-islami*), *shura* Democracy and the implementation of the Shari`a as opposed to Secularism (`*ilmaniyya*), Part 1, *Islam and Christian–Muslim Relations*, 3, 183–210 (Part 2 in *ICMR*, 4, 1993, 83–99).